The Journey Begins

(Recovery of life, of dreams,-of love, of self!)

At

WESTERBROOK CENTER

"Just walk thru the gates"

A sanctuary of hope that is bounded on three sides by the lush forests of the Louisiana bayou with a silent, yet bubbling brook, inexorably coursing its way through the estate that stands as a monument to those who came before and a beacon for those yet to enter its doors: A place where magic happens!

By Dan Cauthorn, Ph.D., L.P.C.

INFINITY PUBLISHING

ISBN 0-7414-5842-X

Printed in the United States of America

Published March 2010

INFINITY PUBLISHING
1094 New DeHaven Street, Suite 100
West Conshohocken, PA 19428-2713
Toll-free (877) BUY BOOK
Local Phone (610) 941-9999
Fax (610) 941-9959
Info@buybooksontheweb.com
www.buybooksontheweb.com

TABLE OF CONTENTS

AUTHOR'S NOTE

If you have ever wanted to know how treatment for chemical dependency occurs, you can begin to understand that process within the pages of this book. It is the point of regaining life for the individual with the dependency. It hurts at times just as life hurts at times but "survival" becomes a rallying cry. Fear of the process shall be replaced with a deeply held belief that treatment works and those professionals who provide and deliver the treatment experience day-to-day expect and observe miracles. Those in the trenches who daily build to provide a platform for recovery and hence, sobriety, deserve our deepest respect and admiration.

This journey into the treatment of addiction spreads across a broad spectrum of substances, actions and thoughts. Other addictions exist! And these addictions create chaos and havoc in the lives of those individuals who must share and co-participate with the person afflicted with the disease. The familial unit, both nuclear and extended members, continues to, in some measure, to blame themselves for the "chaos and havoc."

Though I am presently retired from the addiction treatment and mental-health fields, I remain most thankful for the privilege of participating and observing a life force being re-illuminated, transformed, and re-energized through sustained recovery efforts that are gradually implemented and adopted by the individual. I continue to stand in awe of those treatment providers who remain on the front lines, day-in and day-out, offering and delivering the treatment to those who persevere.

Enjoy the read and listen for the magic to emerge.

FOREWORD

Many years ago the treatment recovery organization I worked for assembled a team known as "Professional Services" to monitor and improve the quality and effectiveness of patient care. Dan and I were members of that team and I have been privileged to be his friend since then. He has worked for decades in several capacities in the addiction field, from counselor to program director to corporate administration to consultant. Rather than focus on what society defines as "success" he chose to leave management to get back to his roots and his passion of working with addicts and alcoholics on reaching recovery one step at a time, one day at a time.

He sets his own standards of care high and expects nothing less of other professionals. He is among the most ethical, honest people I have ever met. Dan is one of those rare people who listens well to both words and body language and can gently guide a person to self-discovery.

One of his gifts is the ability to take disparate chunks of information about a patient and compile a diagnostic summary and from that the blueprint of what the person needs to accomplish to make progress. I am delighted he has put that skill to use in creating this book.

Linda Patton, MBA
Regional VP, Behavioral Health Concepts

DEDICATION

After twenty-plus years of being a service-provider within the substance abuse and mental health industries, it is inevitable that others' thoughts, words, ideas, and practices would appear within the described depictions of recovery. For those of you who may see yourselves within these pages, I extend a deep gratitude to you for being there to teach me and to encourage me on my personal journey; I humbly acknowledge your presence within these pages.

To those who have traveled along that desperate road, I dedicate this story and with a special hope that some young person will pick up this "chip of a book" (Alcoholics Anonymous) when that detour sign approaches and beckons, the better road will have been chosen.

To the two co-founders of Alcoholics Anonymous: Bill W and Dr. Bob,

To those families and significant others who have suffered as a direct result of this insidious disease and found hope for themselves as a result of the Alanon Program and the treatment industry in providing the catalyst.

AND, to my wife, Elizabeth, who continues to love me and remains my very best friend and confidante.

It is time for Jay's story to be told describing his perilous yet naïve journey into and out of the nightmare of chemical dependency. The road toward chemical dependency is lined with fancy advertisements and enticements to a life of freedom, happiness, and joy but the potholes and roadblocks encountered were grandiose lies of allurement embedded within a philosophy of hard work and tenacity.

PREFACE

"My friends, I had not intended to discuss this controversial subject at this particular time. However, I want you to know that I do not shun controversy. On the contrary, I will take a stand on any issue at any time, regardless of how fraught with controversy it might be. You have asked me how I feel about whisky. All right, here is how I feel about whisky: If when you say whisky you mean the devil's brew, the poison scourge, the bloody monster that defiles innocence, dethrones reason, destroys the home, creates misery and poverty, yea literally takes the bread from the mouths of little children; if you mean the evil drink that topples the Christian man and woman from the pinnacles of righteous, gracious living into the bottomless pit of degradation and despair, and shame, and hopelessness, then certainly I am against it. BUT, if when you say whisky, you mean the oil of conversation, the philosophic wine, the ale that is consumed when good fellows get together, that puts a song in their hearts and laughter on their lips and the warm glow of contentment in their eyes; if you mean Christmas cheer; if you mean the stimulating drink that puts the spring in the old gentleman's step on a frosty, crisp morning, if you mean the drink which enables a man to magnify his joy and his happiness, and to forget, if only for a little while, life's great tragedies, and heartbreaks and sorrows; if you mean that drink, the sale of which pours into our treasuries untold millions of dollars, which are used to provide tender care for our little crippled children, our blind, our deaf, our dumb, our pitiful aged and infirm; to build highways and hospitals and schools, then certainly I am for it. This is my stand. I will not retreat from it. I will not compromise."

(The speech is reprinted from The Commercial Appeal (Memphis, TN.), 12 April 1984, p.B2

Somewhere within the subtle words intertwined in the paragraph above, the disease of addiction to alcohol is well described and underscored. Alcoholism is defined as a primary, chronic disease with genetic, psychosocial, and environmental factors influencing its development and manifestations. This disease is progressive and potentially fatal. It is characterized by a lack of control over drinking, preoccupation with the drug alcohol, continued use of alcohol despite adverse consequences, and distortions in thinking, most notable "denial." Each of these symptoms may be continuous or periodic. Alcoholism is "not" the result of a sinful nature, a moral weakness, or a character flaw, nor is it caused by a miserable childhood, a lack of self-control, lack of willpower, or self-centeredness. No alcoholic in the depths of his disease and despair over losses sustained made a conscious decision with the first drink of alcohol to lose his very existence, i.e., "Well, let me consider this: I'm twelve years old and if I work on this drinking thing, I can be a roaring alcoholic and in the gutter of life by age thirty-two." I just do not believe this happens. Treatment is an aspect of the continuing journey into life that points those in need toward recovery of regaining what has been lost to addiction through a continuing series of actions designed specifically for that purpose thus providing them the necessary time to reclaim themselves. Recovery is a gradual "process" and not an "event." It also suggests certain "Steps" (Alcoholics Anonymous) that will lead to continued health and well-being. But it does not guarantee restoration or sobriety! Sobriety emerges where abstinence from addictive chemicals is practiced by each recovering person, one day at a time.

I will attempt, within the pages of this fictional depiction, to portray the true life story of the alcoholic as graphically as possible without destroying the realism of actual events that have unfolded in countless lives of men and women for years. Within the context of the life-story, the process of treatment and the depths of addiction (alcoholism) and recovery will be explored, enhanced, and brought to the light of day from the viewpoint of the patient (the alcoholic) and the family of the alcoholic.

I have chosen a "novel format" as the vehicular approach to delineating and articulating the disease of chemical dependency and the recovery process. This book was born out of my frustration in not locating specific readings relative to the sensitive issues in treating the alcoholic and/or drug addicted individual; what do they do back there, became a commonly asked question, especially from family members and significant others. "Do they hook them up to electrical machines or is religion practiced on them?" One elderly black woman asked, "Will yall drain him?"

This narrative will hold your attention and your heart both on the entertainment and intellectual level. Now you will know "What they do back there?"

One thing is certain. Many alcoholics may never see the light of recovery and the serenity and peace that it promises and neither will the families involved.

This book is meant to interrupt the massive global denial that permeates the whole of society regarding the severity of addictions, whether the drug utilized is alcohol or some other addictive drug or whether it is behaviors involving sex, food, gambling, spending, or work.

Disclaimer: The characters and the locations described and portrayed in this book are fictional and any resemblance to any person, living or dead is purely coincidental. This volume is composed of hundreds of clients that I have been privileged and honored to know and respect. Jay is a character composed of many players in the throes of alcoholism. The process is important but recovery is paramount as this story unfolds. Many who have contributed to the field of chemical dependency provided much in the telling of this story; the journey of death to life! And to all of those wonderful people, I shall always be indebted and grateful.

I also want to extend a special appreciation to Barbara Yarber, RHT, CMT, ABQAVRP who has spent countless hours in the process of editing. She is a very special lady. She has taught me that angels absolutely exist in this world and in our lives!

I, also, want to extend my appreciation to and acknowledge the cooperation of Alcoholics Anonymous World Services, New York City, NY and The Commercial Appeal, Memphis TN.

OVER THE LINE

"Chasing the elusive mystery key along
We rode with the authority of thirty-strong,
Uncaring devotion for this rigid life and
In every turn we caused new strife.

Those and I ran the course
Probing, stopping short -
Somewhere near that hidden line
A place of last resort.

Dashing onward and upward we sought
Our grand thoughts prevailed;
And who would have thought
We had seen the gates of hell!

Over the line myself, twelve and friend
With all life's treasures untold.
Then finding our way back home again
And off we proudly rode!"
(Dan Cauthorn, 1986)

Chapter 1 – In the Beginning

As I drove up the winding drive to the Bienville Estate, I was overwhelmed at the beauty of the grounds. Stately oak trees lined the drive and beautiful magnolia trees dotted the landscape. The azaleas were a splash of colors that any artist would have envied for his palette. As an up and coming reporter for the Southern Heritage magazine, I wondered what kind of reception I would get from the Bienvilles. They were strictly bayou, staunchly southern and very private. Southern Heritage had made several attempts to schedule an interview in the past and my editor was amazed when Jeninne Bienville granted *me* the interview. I was hoping to get a photograph of Mrs. Bienville but had decided not to press the issue if she strongly denied my request.

Just as I was beginning to wonder if I would ever reach the house, it loomed large in front of me. This was decidedly the most impressive house I had ever seen. It was not your typical antebellum mansion. This was a large French chalet done in pastel blue and cream. There was no front porch and the cobblestone walk led you through the green carpet of grass to the front door, which was sheltered by a lattice-enclosed stoop. The spring flowers were lovely. A bed of pansies lay on each side of the walk and continued along the front of the house. There were rose gardens and various evergreen ground covers. An arched trellis covered with lilacs granted entrance to the backgrounds of this breath taking estate.

I rang the doorbell and was greeted by an attractive young woman in a conservative business suit. I told her that I was Delta DuBois and before I could make any further identification she said, "Yes, Mrs. Bienville is expecting you. I am Louisa Mathers, Mrs. Bienville's personal secretary. Follow me please." As we strode across immaculate wooden floors, I noticed the elegant understatement of the room. The creamy rugs accented the deeply polished floor. The sofa was cream with a small raspberry stripe and had pillows in colors ranging from the palest pink to the deepest wine and the elegant loveseat near the window was deep hunter green with cream and raspberry pillows. The two overstuffed chairs were hunter green, cream and raspberry florals. Against the inner wall was a large, dark oak roll top desk and there were a few strikingly beautiful accent pieces. It *was* obvious that there had been quite a cash outlay for this room!

Louisa led me through the living room into a glassed room filled with lovely growing plants and wicker furniture. As we stepped out onto the terrace, the beauty surrounding me faded in the background as Mrs. Bienville stood to greet me. She was a beautiful woman. My research had disclosed her age to be 62 but she didn't look it. Her hair was a deep auburn color. It almost looked black until the sun caught it sending out sparks of copper creating the illusion of a halo around her head. There were white wings at her temples but this was the only place. Her skin was creamy olive and her eyes were black with long curling eyelashes. Her full mouth was her best feature and when it curved into a smile her whole face lit up. She was a tall woman, probably five nine or five ten and full figured without being plump.

"Have a seat Miss DuBois (how did she know I was not married) and Louisa, have Greta bring tea." As Louisa disappeared, Mrs. Bienville turned her charm back to me. "Well," she said, "where do you want to begin?" Her voice was low and melodious and there was a hint of an accent that I could not place.

For me, there was only one place to start. "Tell me about you." "Ah," she said with a small smile, "this should be fun!" I heard the rattling of a teacart, as a young lady appeared, which bore sterling silver tea and coffee services as well as some of the most mouthwatering pastries I had ever seen. "Tea or coffee, Miss DuBois?" As I started to answer she went on to say, "I can't offer you anything stronger. We don't keep spirits here and haven't for quite a while." I assured her coffee was fine and settled with my tape recorder set on ready. She eyed the recorder skeptically and stated that she hoped I was the only one who would listen to her. I dispelled her fears and asked her to begin wherever she wanted.

"Well," she said, "I am not a native of Louisiana. I was born in Cherry Hill, Virginia (the unidentified accent!). My parents and relatives were prominent citizens of the community, that is, until my Father's secret was discovered. I was about thirteen, I guess, when the preacher found out about my Daddy's recipe. Of course, it was moonshine, but the best moonshine anyone ever tasted. I never tasted anyone's except my Daddy's but I can attest that it was mighty fine. The family practically disowned Daddy and the community decided that it would be in everyone's best interest if we left Cherry Hill. Oh, I didn't tell you my maiden name. Well, it is WesterBrook." Mrs. Bienville chuckled, "Close your mouth Miss DuBois, yes; it is the same WesterBrook that has the hospital for drug addicts and alcoholics."

"Delta, my husband and son aren't the only attorneys in this family. I met Charles Bienville when I was a first year law student at Credence School of Law in Baton Rouge. We fell in love and planned to marry after graduation and after we had established our law practices. However, I was two months pregnant with Jay when I graduated and never got to start my law practice. After Jay was born, I drank often and quite regularly. This continued for sometime but I hid it quite well. One afternoon Charles came home to find Jay wailing and me, passed out on the living room floor. He called my Daddy and together they found a place to send me. It was really an awful place and Daddy said he was going to see that people with alcohol problems would have a decent place to go for treatment. Thus, WesterBrook was conceived and born. Some wonderful things take place there, Miss DuBois. Lives are salvaged, lives that most people have long since given up." Delta Dubois looked at Jeninne Bienville and softly, said, "Tell me about your hospitalization."

Jeninne's look became distant, as if she had retreated into a past time and place. She squared her shoulders and looked Delta directly in the eyes.

"I don't know if I can," she stated flatly. Delta thought Mrs. Bienville was going to deny her request but after a minute or two, she began her story: "When I look back I see that my dependence on alcohol began long before I was in law school but I controlled it rather well. My parents did not know I was slipping liquor from the cabinet. I was very careful not to take too much for fear it would be missed. Therefore, I developed a taste for all types of alcohol; whiskey, gin, brandy, and wine. You name it and I could drink it. I drank steadily throughout high school and college but I drank less when I was in law school. Drinking robbed me of my ability to concentrate and made me fuzzy-minded. Also I had met Charles. But when I became pregnant I knew Charles and I had to get married. You must realize that in those days, in the prim and proper town of LaPorte, there was absolutely no other alternative. Charles was wonderful and steadily said that once the baby was born; I could turn my attention to establishing my law practice. However, when Jay was one year old, I realized that it would never happen, because there were too many demands made on me socially. It was expected, that I, as Charles' wife, would raise his children, preside over his house and totally support him on a professional and social level. I began my serious drinking at this point.

More than once I embarrassed Charles but he was at a loss as to what should be done. Jay was fifteen months old when Charles came in to find me drunk on the floor. My Father arrived shortly after Charles' call and they decided to admit, or perhaps "commit" is a better word, me to Hedgewood Psychiatric Hospital. Back in the early '50s there were no specialized treatment centers for alcoholics, we were simply admitted to hospitals for the insane! People, including the medical world, viewed alcoholism as a moral weakness rather than a disease. If "we" would just go to church, confess our sin, and stop drinking all would be well; we would be forgiven and welcomed back into our family, community and social world! If only it was that simple.

I awoke in the hospital. I did not know where I was and was terribly disoriented. I gradually noticed that I was not on a bed, but rather a padded platform that was actually a part of the wall and floor. There was no furniture in the room. Room! I was in a padded cell! I looked down and realized I had on only a cotton hospital gown (and even it was taken away as I began my withdrawal symptoms). Shortly a nurse came in and asked me if I knew where I was and how I got there. I told her "no" and asked for an answer to her question. She simply grunted and said the doctor would be in soon and he would explain everything. By the time the doctor got around to visiting me, I was well into withdrawal and he merely looked into the room and left. For forty-eight hours I screamed, shook, saw spiders and bugs, threw up and sweated. During this time no one even gave me a drink of water, not that I could have kept it down. They gave me nothing to ease my symptoms of alcohol withdrawal. I had been at Hedgewood six days before I knew where I was and why I was there. I underwent aversion therapy as well as shock treatment. I was made to drink until I got physically ill from the alcohol and then was made to drink more. If that part of my "treatment" wasn't bad enough, shock treatment was a nightmare. I was not given any type of sedative before the treatment was given. I was strapped down to the table, a tongue depressor was inserted in my mouth and for all practical purposes, I was electrocuted! It was my stay at Hedgewood that ended any hope of getting a law practice started. I am sure their intentions were for my best, but they knew so little then.

Anyway, Jay was six years old before I felt competent enough to be left alone with him. Today, I still have parts of my memory that have been permanently erased by the shock treatments I received. I was in the hospital six months. During this time, I had weekly sessions with the doctor and a few planned activities. Not once during this whole time did I ever have the opportunity to talk, in a group setting, or with another person there for alcohol related reasons. No one mentioned Alcoholics Anonymous nor suggested that I attend meetings. I did not attend an AA meeting until a little over two years ago when my son was in treatment at WesterBrook. This is a part of their recovery program. Now he and I attend weekly meetings. How I wish I had known all those years ago. I wouldn't have felt so alone. For the record, Miss DuBois, I have not had an alcoholic drink in over 40 years. It has not been easy and I don't think of it as 40 years of sobriety. It is a day-to-day thing. Today, I have chosen not to drink. Tomorrow, I will have to choose again. I hope I will choose not to drink, but at least, I do have a choice in the matter. There was a time when I had none, the only thing I could do was drink."

Delta looked at her face. Jeninne Bienville had a look of serenity and the quiet dignity a person exhibits when she has been on the brink of insanity, has looked over the edge, and chosen not to leap. Delta was snatched out of her thoughts by a loud booming "Mother, where are you?" Mrs. Bienville smiled, and said, "That will be Charles; he always calls me mother." A very tall, slim, tanned man with silver white hair poked his head around the lilac trellis and beamed when he saw his wife's smile. Delta was aware that for Charles Bienville, the only woman visible was his wife. He kissed her gently. "Hello my darling," she said, "This is Miss Delta DuBois. Miss DuBois is a reporter for the Southern Heritage Magazine. She is here doing a story on us." Please be as gentle with your remarks."

Charles said, "Don't rattle too many family skeletons, Miss DuBois; you know how this part of the state is! We might have to leave," as he winked at Jeninne and left. I turned to her, "You must tell me about Charles." Although it had seemed to Delta that this lady was as beautiful as one could be, at the mention of Charles' name, Jeninne's face became illuminated. The play of emotions was spellbinding. Her eyes flashed love, humor, passion, and obsession! Her smile spoke commitment, tolerance, indulgence, in a word, forever and ever! Delta knew this was Jeninne's favorite topic and settled back to hear. "I met Charles during our first year of law school, she began. He was decidedly the most personable man I had ever met. He is quite tall, you know, well over six feet five inches tall. His silver hair was black then, black as a crow's wing. He has always been slender and thank goodness Jay takes after him in that respect!" I am constantly watching my weight. Anyway, back to Charles. "When I first saw him I thought he was good looking but when I met him, boy, did our personalities clash. I did not like Charles Bienville and made no attempt to hide it. Perhaps that was what interested me the most. Young women were constantly throwing themselves at him. My distance must have been a novelty for him. But at any rate, he began his pursuit and I, my flight into the game! I really don't think Charles meant to fall in love with me and I certainly had no intention along those lines. Charles was serious about one thing: His law studies. I played with my studies. Charles turned that around for me. I began to take a real interest in the academics of the courses. Charles and I became good friends and I found out that he was the youngest son of "the Bienville Family of LaPorte". This meant wealth but it was not important to me. I found I could share feelings and thoughts with him that I had never shared with anyone before. One evening we were debating a tort case we were to brief for the next day and the debate turned into friendly horseplay. As we tussled on the floor the touches became softer and more intimate. I can honestly say I had never made love with anyone before Charles. He must have felt the same way because our thoughts were spoken in unison "incredible"! Don't get the impression that after that evening we were in the bed every time we were alone. It just didn't happen that way. We went about the business of falling in love slowly. I hadn't given much thought to birth control until Charles mentioned it. He said "Jeannie I know we would produce the most incredible child but we should wait until we have graduation behind us, have our law practices established and are married." "This was the first mention of marriage. It rather astounded me but as I thought about it, I knew we both were aware that it just had to be that way. There was no one else for either of us. We had tried that route before. We would meet and discuss our "date" with the other. Finally, we agreed it was simply a waste of time. We wanted to be with each other and that was that. I knew Charles was right about the child so I suggested that I get fitted for a diaphragm. Charles said he had read up on those things and that they were only slightly more effective than a condom and rather than my having to submit to an embarrassing physician exam, he would take care of the birth control measure. Charles was very responsible. The fact that I got pregnant had nothing to do with his failure to take precaution. We were just caught in that 30% failure ratio. When I found out that I was going to have a baby, Charles was absolutely wonderful. He said this was going to be a very special baby and must have been meant to be. We had the traditional wedding and I am sure people began counting up days and months when my expectancy was announced. Charles started his law practice in LaPorte. We didn't have the usual struggles young attorneys have. Charles had wealth and that meant he could not only support his family but could do community work as well. Over the years Charles has taken cases where the clients couldn't possibly pay. As a matter of fact, the majority of his clients were LaPorte's down-and-outers. People whose families and society had given up on. He held legal seminars, community workshops and anything else he could come up with to give to the community. He never neglected his family responsibilities nor did he make me feel inferior because of my disease and inability to practice law. He apologized to me for the social commitments his law practice demanded of me. Two years ago Charles retired from the bench. Now he does consultant work and still is involved in community service. He is also beginning to repair his relationship with Jay. Charles loves me more than any other person living and that includes his son. Charles was a good father and spent more than average time with Jay. But when we were together, it was obvious to everyone including Jay, that Charles was devoted to me. I always suspected that Jay felt left out when we were together as a family. I tried to draw him into the circle but his father seemed to intimidate him although Jay constantly vied for his father's approval and attention. Maybe since Jay feels about Kayce like his father feels about me, he can understand his father better. Maybe Charles is beginning to understand Jay a little better also. Time will tell. I tell you, Miss BuBois, being a wife and mother is not an easy task. However, it is immensely rewarding."

Delta looked at her watch, good lord, had four hours already passed. She had arrived around 9:00 A.M. and it was already one o'clock. With a measure of guilt she looked at Mrs.Bienville. "Geeze, I have kept you talking through your lunch. I know good manners say I should leave now, but,

Mrs. Bienville, I simply must have you tell me about Jay. Could I come back tomorrow?" Silver laughter bubbled out of Jeninne's throat. "Miss DuBoise, if you will follow me into the Florida room you will find lunch has been prepared and is waiting for us. Greta signaled me about ten minutes ago. After we eat, we will take a stroll in the back gardens, after that, I will tell you about my child."

The wicker table in the Florida room was set for three. A tablecloth of peacock blue linen had been added. Placemats and napkins were of matching floral colors. The day china was pale yellow with a peacock blue rim. The glasses were stemmed crystal. Sterling silver flatware graced the settings.

Charles entered the room and first seated Jeninne and then me. Greta served us tomato aspic followed by a platter of cold roast breast of chicken, a relish tray, condiment tray, and an assortment of sliced breads. Two crystal pitchers held iced spring water and iced tea. Luncheon conversation was light and the Bienvilles seemed genuinely interested in my presence and asked meaningful questions. I never got the impression that we were holding "polite" conversation. Afterward Greta brought dessert and coffee (almond cream torte and a rich Cajun blend coffee); Charles gave Jeninne a quick kiss and excused himself.

Louisa Mathers appeared and informed Mrs. Bienville that correspondence was completed and only lacked her signature, the social calendar for the upcoming month arranged and telephone calls returned. Mrs. Bienville thanked Louisa and dismissed her for the day.

As we strolled along the back gardens, I became increasingly aware that the social community probably did not know the Bienvilles I had met this day. Charles and Jeninne were not the least bit snobbish. Indeed, they excelled in making a perfect stranger feel at home. Briefly I considered that this was a contrived appearance strictly for my benefit but I dismissed it as quickly as I had entertained it. They were too relaxed with each other and with me, the house was too well run and Greta and Louisa were "real". No, I was seeing the genuine Charles and Jeninne. I was delighted with this conclusion.

As we headed back to the terrace, Jeninne began to talk about Jay. "Jay was born November 23, 1952. He was a good baby although my recollection of his early years is sketchy. I had a Nanny who took care of him until he was five years old. Mrs. Nesbitt was a grandmotherly type who took to Jay immediately. She referred to alcoholism as my "condition" and was very protective of both Jay and me. She died ten years ago. Charles, Jay, and I attended her funeral. Looking back, Mrs. Nesbitt spoiled Jay. Perhaps it was because she recognized the bond between Charles and me and knew Jay felt left out. I am sure Jay grew up lonely because Charles and I did not have any more children. By the time I felt physically and mentally well enough for another baby, Jay was eight years old. Although we did try, we were unable to have another child.

We tried to encourage a normal childhood for Jay. Sometimes coming from a very wealthy family puts a child at a disadvantage. Charles, at times, would delay a request by Jay explaining the item was too expensive. Of course expense was not the issue, but wanting Jay to fit in with the other children in school was. Also, Jay's lack of self-esteem made him a prime candidate for friends who wanted to be friends with Jay's money rather than with Jay himself.

There were two youngsters who we were thankful chose Jay for friendship. Jon Moreau who was, and today remains, Jay's best friend. Jon and Jay are the same age. Then, there was Kayce McClary. Kayce and Jay have been married nine years now. Kayce admired Jay and followed him around as a child; she is five years younger than Jay. These two anchored

Jay. Jon kept his feet on the ground and Kayce's innocent trust and adoration stopped Jay from some things that he ordinarily would have done. Anyway, these two helped Jay have a relatively normal childhood.

Jay had the typical teen years, if being a teen in the late '60s and early '70s had any normality. We were thankful that, except for one experiment with pot, Jay did not use drugs. Since we kept no liquor in the house, it never occurred to us that he drank to excess. Of course, we knew about the "beer parties" but since he showed no signs of alcohol abuse in our household we assumed this was a phase which would pass by the time he was out of college and law school. Had we known then of the genetic aspect of the disease of alcoholism, we would have been frantic!

Jay was not a Mamma's boy. Actually, he was reserved when it came to display of affection. I suppose that came from his believing that he could not compete nor be accepted into the affectionate bond between his Father and me. He seemed to maintain a love-hate relationship with me and his father, especially his father. Jay enjoyed manipulating Charles. He was most happy when he thought he had bested Charles. Yet, it was important to him that Charles approve of the things he did. Any show of disapproval by his father devastated Jay. But rather than show how hurt he was, Jay went hell-bent into whatever caused Charles to disapprove. I remember once, when Jay was in college, Charles was quite verbal about a young woman Jay was seeing. Shelby Longmire was a woman with questionable morals. She was quite lovely and had a string of males following her all the time, like a bitch in heat! And, she was not particular whom she slept with. Rather than try to talk with Charles about it, Jay did his usual retreat and quite openly, to spite his Father, continued to associate with Shelby. As a matter of fact, up until three years ago, Jay continued his immoral relationship with Shelby, even though he married Kayce.

Miss DuBois, it is a shame, but for all his money, position and power, my son lived a perfectly miserable life until he almost lost everything as a result of an automobile accident. Sometimes God takes the back way to reach us. I suppose that is what he did with Jay. Jay has a story of his own to tell. Perhaps someday he will."

Jeninne Bienville turned her head and looked across the sculptured terraces and well designed gardens, I knew our interview had drawn to a close. I risked one last request. "Mrs. Bienville, may I have a photograph of you for my article?" "Certainly, my dear, I would be pleased to do that for you. I have shared some of the Bienville and WesterBrook's most intimate secrets. Why not have a photograph!"

As I left the Bienville estate, I watched the sun settle behind the horizon. I realized that I was exhausted. This had been one of the most exciting days of my life. I was eager to begin the journey.

Chapter 2 – Jay's Story

Ordinarily sleep was a special gift from the gods but tonight Jay's sleep was interrupted by tossing and turning and that chilling dream again. He abruptly sat up in bed somewhat disoriented and strangely afraid. "Kayce is sleeping soundly and peacefully and here I am wide wake because of that same damn dream," he thought to himself. He abruptly turned back the covers and slid his feet onto the plush, carpeted floor. The alarm clock reflecting 3:30AM on the night stand caught his eye and the brightness of the displayed time seemed to mock him. He slowly made his way to the bathroom and sat down with his head in his hands, half-awake and half-asleep. He lit his first cigarette for the day and inhaled deeply. His chest tightened with the rush. The taste was gone but his body demanded the stimulant-like effect. This morning's experience was not unlike many others, so many in fact, he did not want to contemplate them. His mouth felt as if he had been eating cotton all night and he knew what a cool drink of water would do for that. The ashes fell off the end of his cigarette onto the tile floor and that silently angered him. He pondered silently to himself in the half-light of the early morning. "Is this all?" He quickly downed two Motrin and returned to Kayce's side. She stirred quietly as he touched her shoulder and sighed softly as he snuggled next to her. The alarm clock sounded almost immediately and his day began again.

His morning routine resurfaced as countless others had done. As he showered, the rich aroma of brewing coffee assailed his senses. He stepped out of the shower, wrapped the towel around his waist, went to the kitchen and poured himself a steaming mug. He felt queasy and uneasy as he returned to the bedroom to dress. His headache was lurking nearby and it was ever so slowly raising its ugly but familiar face. Kayce remained in bed and mumbled a half-hearted "morning" and he simply replied, "yeah." He left the house without further comment and headed for his office downtown. The sun was shining brightly and that seemed to perk him up somewhat. Another day he thought.

As he stepped out of his car in the garage parking area, he saw a familiar and easily recognizable figure walking slowly and unsteadily down the street with his collar turned up against the cool, morning air. Damn, that's pathetic: He's drunk again. Something needs to be done about keeping those drunks off the street, he mumbled to himself. He impatiently punched the elevator button and ascended to his plush office overlooking the town square. He was the first one there so he went to the employee lounge to make the coffee. For a fleeting moment he wondered why seeing old McGreggor irritated him so. For some reason, and he did not want to pursue it, he knew it was fear. He immediately dismissed all thoughts of the drunken old man and returned to his office with a cup of coffee.

As he sat at his desk reviewing the agenda for the day, his secretary rang through, "The Mayor on line one, Jay." Mechanically and with a familiar "what now" attitude he reached for the telephone and pushed the button, "yes, Mayor." After what seemed an eternity, he re-cradled the phone and slumped back in his chair. He spun around slowly in his chair to stare out the window. Will that man ever understand, slowly crept into Jay's thoughts. The sun continued to brightly shine but he considered, "not for him." His enthusiasm for this plush job was waning all too rapidly. I need a drink, he thought automatically. Also, again the thought, Is this all there is?

The telephone rang again as Jay sat in his office reviewing the briefs before him. Kayce wanted to know what time to expect him home. She had decided to prepare Jay's favorite meal and wanted everything just right. "Kayce, I cannot think about food right now. I am knee-deep in paperwork on this damn case. Don't wait for me; I'll see you when I get home. Okay?"

Kayce knew it was useless to prod him further and she acquiesced. "Okay, see you then." She was hurt but didn't say anything else. Jay hung up the telephone returning to the case that had haunted him for months. The case was getting out of control and it seemed to be slipping out of his grasp. Additional assistance was needed but Jay in his perfectionism and egomania attitude couldn't find the courage to seek outside help. It was getting late and again he decided to visit Budde's for a cool drink and then a return to his work. That would clear the "cobwebs" from his mind.

After arriving at Budde's, Shelby brought him a drink and she tried to engage him in small talk, but to no avail. He was preoccupied with the case and nothing else really mattered. He downed the bourbon and water Shelby had served him, and quickly ordered a double. As Jay sat nursing the drink, Tommy Venable walked through the front door.

Tommy was a rough-looking man with cold-dark eyes with his hair pulled back into a ponytail. He had been "fragged" while serving in Vietnam resulting from an incident involving the death of several Special Forces members of his platoon even though he had been warned of the ambush by the South Vietnamese Ranger Scouts. He was a "gung-ho" macho-type but now walked with a rather pronounced limp as a result; one might say a very unsavory character but the investigator Jay needed right now. A plan was incubating in Jay's thoughts.

These types of administrative cases were tricky at times and the City of LaPorte couldn't afford to lose this case. Workman's Compensation cases that get to court were always difficult because nine out of ten were either neck or back injuries sustained in the line of duty. These were difficult to disprove because the matter of pain which was felt by the plaintiff was difficult to measure by the court. Since x-rays never revealed felt pain or its degree of severity, Jay felt assured of a tight case. Jay had hit upon an idea to hire Tommy to get footage with the camcorder that clearly would prove "non-disability" and thus save the city of LaPorte big dollars. He motioned to Tommy to come over to his table. Into the night they sat and made elaborate plans including more "cool drinks." He had forgotten about home and Kayce. The deal was struck. Tommy would use an old Chevrolet van and set up the 24-hour surveillance immediately.

Day after day and hour after hour passed, without incident Tommy was beginning to re-experience the fatigue he once knew well. These nightly vigils provided a special opportunity for self-reflection and Tommy certainly had a need to reflect and resolve. His life had changed dramatically upon returning stateside after his tour of duty in the Vietnam fiasco. Promoted to the rank of Captain after two months in the field, being assigned to command a Ranger Reconnaissance Team (a very elitist group!), and his youthful vigor for life coupled with his "gung-ho mentality," all of these combined to instill the "consummate professional soldier".

Rangers as advisors and consultants, hell! He knew why he had come to this war and that was to kill the enemy! His ambitions and high regard for life had once been "apple pie and the heartbeat of America" but somehow part of him had died in the jungles and rice paddies of Southeast Asia. The drugs he theorized easily assisted in soothing the relentless emotional pain within his soul but nothing to remove the scar tissue, the pain he carried and endured as he had been taught to endure. He was always on the "edge" and falling was his constant companion. He readily acknowledged the edge of insanity within his scarred memories. He felt betrayed and abandoned by the rhetoric of the "apple pie and heartbeat of America" propaganda portrayed by the media. As he sat alone with the quiet of night and his relentless, intrusive thoughts, he silently reflected the errors and terrors of his Vietnam experience. In the silence of the dark night, he wondered had he fallen already into an acceptance of a mediocre existence!

Old tapes of the smell of war, of hideous wounds and the loss of innocence, the dust and mud, the snakes, leeches, the constant vigilance and stress, the acrid smell of jet fuel, the "rap, rap, rap" of the "choppers," and always the peculiar smell of blood. Heroin and its magic played louder than all of the deadening harsh reality of his present existence. This "joint" would have to do for now and he inhaled deeply.

A movement in the viewfinder stirred him from his foggy ruminations and the attention to the last hit of the "roach." This was the opportunity needed and all of it came out beautifully on the VCR. Tommy's hurried and excited call to Jay brought feelings of the "conquering hero." This would please everyone except of the course, the plaintiff in the case. Jay's plan had worked to perfection.

As the court proceedings reconvened, Jay purposely played the "Columbo" role to set up the scenario of using the videocassette tape. The plaintiff and his attorney sat smug certain in the knowledge they could not lose this long and drawn out case.

The TV and VCR were wheeled into the courtroom with prior approval by the Court. Jay masterfully set the scene and switched the machines to the "on" position. The cassette tape began to whirl out doom for the plaintiff; neck-brace and all! It was over and everyone knew it. This case had gone back and forth for over nine months and now when the gavel fell "today," it would be over and a victory for him.

Congratulations were exchanged as Jay headed back to his office. He sat feeling rather smug about himself and his magnificent performance.

Watching intensely as the minute hand inched and ticked toward his designated "quitting time," Jay had convinced himself that this day's work really deserved to be celebrated. He had just won a much publicized workman's compensation case and his checking account balance would surely validate his successful handling of the case. Jay was well known for equating success in life in terms of money and material possessions. He would share his victory and shining moment with others and bask in the certain knowledge that he had indeed "arrived." Indeed.

He had thoughts and visions of this glorious moment of his every waking hour. This had been the internal motivation that had propelled him. What had been holding him back? What had he been doing wrong? These questions concerned him greatly and they refused to give him rest and peace.

Others had, at times, remarked how clever he was in the courtroom and how well he made use of his intellectual abilities and clarity of thought. However, he was unable to sustain these bursts and he would lose interest and lose sight of the goal just within his reach. He would continue to dream and build and then without reason would bring the project down around him directly as a result of his impatience and his inability to follow through on a timely basis.

This time it was different and he knew it! This time, others would know it also! The rest of the crowd at work, his associates and friends, had always congregated at Beau's Paux, a "Frenchie" little bar and grill, very plush and upbeat where only certain successful well-doers frequented. Certainly now he had found his niche. Secretly he felt second-rate and incompetent: He had survived in this cut-throat business only because of his "highly respected father."

How was it that his father had thrown many rocks during his illustrative career and managed to evade all appearances of wrong-doing! Jay credited being politically correct as the expedient expression of success and dismissed further thoughts of his "highly respected father." He could not live up to those expectations anyway and this realization bore deeply into his heart and soul. He had walked in that mighty shadow for years. Maybe this much-deserved victory would throw illumination into that shadow and forever it would disappear. He could then walk in the light that "he" had created!

When he arrived everyone congratulated him with the results of the difficult case and drink after drink was consumed as the celebration continued. The attitude of those gathered around him was unconditional acceptance. Acceptance by his peers and friends alike was extremely satisfying and a necessity for Jay or so he thought.

The thought of sharing this victory with Kayce never entered into his consciousness. "First things first" was his eternal and continued motto. He would talk with her in the morning over their coffee. The clock was racing now but Jay had no need to be aware of time. As drink after drink was ordered and consumed, the alcohol began to impair his otherwise good judgment. Ordinarily, he was not one to be loud and boisterous, but this night was different and made for celebrating. A great time to celebrate and let his hair down; a good occasion, indeed! His companions were loud, but he rationalized this was a party and "his shining moment."

He also had the idea but maybe not in such a grand place as Beau's Paux. In short order, he and his companions were told to calm down because other patrons were beginning to complain. This chastisement by the establishment angered Jay immediately and he had a thought to really give them a piece of his mind. Who the hell are they anyway? Jay's best friend, Jon, pulled him aside and he calmed down somewhat. He wished his companions and "those others" well, in a sarcastic manner, and decided to move "his" party elsewhere. No one else joined him in his decision to move the party but instead left quietly to their cars and left behind "their" night of celebration. He had urged Jon to go with him but "his best friend" decided to go home instead.

What a "pansy," Jay thought.

Walking out of Beau's Paux Jay signaled to the brightly dressed valet to bring his car around.

Rain begins to mist the late evening air. The young valet roared the car to a stop and opened the door for him. Jay felt it inappropriate but said nothing to the valet. His passive nature was becoming more evident now. The thought stayed with him and teased him about not speaking up at the time. What right did that valet have to "race" his car's finely tuned engine? Damn! The cool night air began to take its toll on Jay and the thought to "not drive" crossed his mind but his ego refused to give up the keys.

He roared out into the night, headed for the bar where he always sought the oblivion of drink and where celebrations were allowed and welcomed, the more the merrier. He would show them in grand style. He arrived, parked his car on the curb and stumbled toward the front entrance. He then went inside and eyed the group assembled at the bar. This was Budde's and definitely not Beau's Paux but Jay loved the light atmosphere and gaiety of the assembled crowd and definitely others would be present to celebrate his success with him as drinks were ordered and re-ordered.

A dimly lit table in the corner was what he needed now. The young, shapely waitress/hostess waved toward him as Jay sauntered into the bar. Jay didn't see the young woman wave at him when he entered the bar. This was Shelby. She was a rather tall brunette with great legs and a figure to match. Her natural disposition was pleasant and out-going. She was a social person who could make friends and acquaintances rather effortlessly. She was at times provocative, at all times sensual and sexual, especially with her short skirts and high heels. Her dark complexion and her round brown eyes completed the picture. She had met Jay many years ago and he, almost naturally and nonchalantly, had continued the relationship even though he married and continued to be married to Kayce. Shelby was the "eternal optimist" in the sense that she never gave up hope that one day she and Jay would be married. Shelby continued to see Jay as often as she could get away and that was that! Shelby always noticed when Jay entered the bar and as he proceeded to his favorite table, she ordered for him. Bringing the drink to the table, the thought crossed her mind of the many nights they had experienced. A mixture of love, concern, and anger clouded any thoughts that intruded as she neared his table. It was apparent that Jay was drunk but she served the drink anyway and sat down beside him. His mood was deceptive as he told her to: Get the hell away!" Tonight she saw very quickly that he was in a vicious mood and she quietly obeyed with no further discussion.

Shelby felt a twinge of pain combined with a strange aloneness as she coolly returned to the kitchen area. After several more drinks, he stumbled to his car and roared off into the night toward home. Shelby, through tear-filled eyes, watched helplessly as the taillights of the sports car disappeared in the distant night. She had known Jay for several years; back to his early college years, the spring breaks, and summer vacations. Shelby longed for a solid relationship with Jay but was now beginning to recognize that any kind of a relationship with Jay was just a distant illusion. But it still hurt and she loved him.

Powering along through the dark night thoughts returned to his shabby behavior and treatment directed toward Shelby. What prompted him to say such a terrible thing to Shelby? Remembered good times flooded his memory. He recalled simpler and fun times with Shelby. He had always felt free and easy around her and they always had a good time. An urge to turn around and return to apologize to Shelby nagged him. But it was getting "late" and he figured maybe "later" on he would apologize for his rude behavior this night.

The road was smooth and straight ahead Jay reasoned and it was getting late! His digital clock indicated 2:45 AM and 6:00 AM was approaching fast. The road is clear tonight, he remarked to himself as the engine responded instantly to his command. Only the whine of the turbocharger intruded into his drunken stupor as his speed increased. Jay watched the speedometer making sure his radar detector was operating properly. Seventy-five miles per hour was acceptable he thought given the conditions of the road. He always had great pride in his driving ability and after several drinks his reflexes were even sharper as his indicated speed increased to eighty-five. His high-speed suspension system responded like a well-oiled perpetual motion machine and with those new Goodyears installed all around, he felt comfortable and secure with his high-speed tactics. He also commented to himself that installing those side-stabilizers was a good investment because they gave the car a solid feel for the road. As Jay continued, the rhythm of the windshield wipers were slowly, but methodically, lulling him into a false sense of security in this most dreadfully dangerous situation. His 3000GT was performing as promised by the dealership as he continued toward his destiny this rainy night in the depths of the Louisiana bayou country. Little did he realize how his life would be forever changed after this "run for home". However, those things beyond the control of man or beast such as the weather had a turn by its own decision and bigger rain droplets began to fall; slowly at first and then a regular pelting of the windshield. He refused to recognize the impending danger and kept his pace toward home. The amount of alcohol he had ingested had taken over his otherwise good senses. The scene was complete with all ingredients and ready to be consummated. Jay did not realize this deadly combination quickly enough to compensate for the long winding curve ahead. The halogen light system installed specifically for this machine brightly lit up the road ahead. He felt the rear tires break their traction and it was much too late to react. Around and around the car screamed until an abrupt stop and unconsciousness for Jay.

As the car slowly came to a grinding halt, the eerie reflection of lights from thousands of particles of glass filled and surrounded the dark road and the crash site.

Jay was unconscious but he was caught between that which is apparent to all present and that which is present to only the involved individual. Saturday morning would never dawn quite the same again as the sheriff and the newly appointed deputy approached the car.

Sheriff Townsend stood well over six feet, five inches tall, a big man, who always wore a black suit, white shirt, and a black bow tie. He reminded one of a mortuary director at a fancy funeral home. He had known Jay for the past twenty-two years and they had indulged in drinks together on more than one occasion. Tonight was no social occasion for either of these two professionals. Sheriff Townsend was focused intently on the accident and he could be very intimidating!

Jay was slumped over in the seat with a warm, sticky liquid running down his cheeks. He could hear those outside and someone in the crowd of rubber-neckers said, "there's no hurry, he's dead!"

This revelation stunned Jay's senses and he screamed within his mind that it was just not true. He clamored for consciousness but none of his limbs would respond appropriately to his commands. Slowly as consciousness slipped back to him, he was able to move his head and the deputy observed the movement. A flurry of activity then erupted around him. A loud whirring noise was heard and his sports car rocked on its tires as the "jaws of Life" ripped into its now lifeless body.

Finally he was out of the car with only a small cut to his scalp. Blood was everywhere and the Emergency Medical Technician remarked, "he's lost a great deal of blood!" The paramedics checked him over and found no other impairment except for the strong odor of alcohol. The EMT further commented that Jay's vital signs were slightly elevated. The "unconsciousness" was probably attributed to an alcohol-induced stupor. The Sheriff discussed Jay's medical condition with the EMT who had performed the assessment. "He's fine Sheriff, except for being quite drunk," the EMT offered.

At this point, the Sheriff then had some rather specific instructions for Jay. Jay was standing near the patrol cruiser when the Sheriff approached. Jay was fumbling in his pocket for a cigarette. He finally retrieved the cigarette and the Sheriff offered him a light. "Thanks," Jay said in a subdued tone of voice. Jay knew the Sheriff was both troubled and angry. He was asked to walk in a straight line and touch his nose with the index finger of his out-stretched hand. Jay tried to follow the instructions but found that he was unable to walk the line as the sheriff had instructed him to do. He stumbled around and sure did attempt to prove, to that sheriff and others around him, that he was not drunk and could handle his liquor as well as any man who walked the bayou country

The sheriff, a longstanding friend of Jay, really did not want to arrest him but those who had gathered to rubberneck were whispering. The Sheriff knew the situation for Jay would be very bad and for his own good he made a decision. He told the Deputy to place Jay in the back seat of the Trace Parish Patrol car and the deputy sheriff was then instructed to transport Jay to the Parish jail in LaPorte. The Sheriff wanted Jay away from the scene as rapidly as possible. The ambulance attendants were just removing the young woman from the other twisted automobile; an extremely traumatic event for the young mother of three who was a Registered Nurse in the Intensive Care Unit at the local hospital in LaPorte. Jay knew nothing about the other person that was involved in the accident. He had no recollection of another car being involved. He could not walk the damn line and his mind kept racing back to the beginning. Still Jay had no awareness of the seriousness of the accident.

He sat on the edge of the concrete culvert still nursing his now throbbing head and waited. The deputy approached with a very authoritarian attitude and said directly to Jay, "Let's go." The deputy opened the back door of the cruiser and assisted Jay in getting into the back seat. "Buckle your seatbelt," the deputy snapped. Jay was able to obey the request but did find it difficult to manipulate the clasp and locking mechanism of the seat belt.

Jay, seated in the back seat of the patrol cruiser, displayed a blank facial expression as if physically and mentally stunned by the events of the past hour. He could see the activity outside of the patrol cruiser and those milling about. Why all this for a simple spin-out and bent-up car, he pondered out loud. His head continued to hurt.

The deputy got into the car and headed toward LaPorte which was ten miles away. No conversations were initiated by either and owing to that, sleep consumed Jay quickly. At the first traffic light, Jay was jarred back to consciousness and his mind begins to race. He had visited the Sheriff's

Department many times during his legal career but never in the context that he presently found himself. Jay, by this time, was experiencing a glimmer of shame and embarrassment. The deputy continued to make no comment and Jay was left with his own thoughts regarding the deputy's non-communicative attitude.

Arriving at the jail, the deputy helped Jay in getting out of the patrol cruiser and escorted him to a holding cell.

Thus far, no one spoke of any legal charges against him. In all this, a thought hit him regarding the disposition of his car but no opportunity presented itself to ask the question. The deputy accompanied Jay to the holding area and opened the big metal door to the cell and motioned mechanically for him to enter. He obediently entered the cell and took two steps forward, when the big metal door clanged shut behind him.

Again he had heard that noise before but not on this side of the bars. After what seemed an eternity for him and after much pacing back and forth trying to piece all this together, he sat down on the edge of the bare cot and smoked a cigarette. A thought intruded of having a drink and how comforting it would be. This thought intrusion frightened him and he didn't know why. Bits and pieces of the past two hours played in his mind like an old movie, slow motion at times, an almost surreal experience. Thoughts of previous mishaps entered to haunt his fragmented present.

As he slowly pulled himself up from the cot, he thought to himself, "never again." Jay did not deal with situations easily and he regressed to simplistic behaviors and attitudes in rationalizing the current events. He went over to the caged window and peered out into the early morning. The superficial injury to his scalp continued to sting and annoys him. His thoughts returned to the beginning as the red and blue lights of the patrol car and ambulance glimmered, danced, and glowed in the background with the distinct smell of rubber and asphalt lingering in the cool morning air. With two DUI convictions over the past six months, Jay had convinced himself and others that never again would he drink and drive, but this occasion proved otherwise. It seemed at times he had a kindred spirit looking after him. Again consequences for his erratic and dangerous behaviors were non-existent until now. But to the extent that deep within, Jay strongly disliked being dependent upon others to rescue him and had come to almost resent those who helped. Over a period of time he was able to resolve that issue and slowly, insidiously came to expect the "enabling" and smoothing over of consequences. "The world owed him anyway!" This became his method of rationalizing the difficulty into obscurity and therefore repressing the shame and guilt that had become a way of life for Jay Bienville.

Today Jay realized that something was drastically wrong!

The incident continued to haunt him and he suspected something more than a wrecked car was involved from the pained facial expression that was directed toward him by the Sheriff of Trace Parish. Solitude seldom lent time for thoughtful reflection and perhaps this was a way for him to cope with life's ups and downs. Jay was simply a "re-actor" as he made his way through life with little to no thought of consequences. What of the consequences? Privately he knew. Always looking inside but never being there. An "outsider" privately but the facade of complete control and self-confidence was polished brightly each day. Each time he would return to the relationship he knew better than any other: Drinking. He reasoned that "it" never failed him! Jay's basic nature matured into a defensive and angrily aggressive stature rather than an appropriate assertive one. Within the confines of his rationalizations, he was beginning to lose himself.

The deputy banging his nightstick on the bars jarred Jay back to the present situation. "You have a visitor," he said tersely.

Jay could then hear the footsteps coming down the hallway. Who could that be, he thought to himself. He looked up and saw Jon standing there with a disappointed and hurt expression on his face. The bars that separated these two friends were an embarrassment for both. Jay could barely maintain eye contact with Jon. After a couple of difficult minutes, Jon asked cautiously, "Can I help you in any way?" He and Jay had been through many scrapes in the past but now he did not know! Jon seemed stunned as Jay glanced up toward him and said, "No, I guess not." Jon pursued his initial question again. "Can I call Kayce for you or your parents?" Jon saw that Jay was hurting and he suspected that the majority of the hurt was shame and embarrassment. Jon thought, "If only Jay knew what really happened last night." Again Jay's response was negative and almost sullen. Jon again decided to push further and asked what had happened. Jay suddenly realized that he had only partial recollection of the events last night. He had suffered a situation very familiar to the alcoholic. He had finally experienced a "blackout," a common symptom of the disease of alcoholism. He could remember leaving Beau's Paux and the misting rain but nothing else came through. The rest of the evening was lost forever in the depths of his mind. He calmly and quickly fabricated the night's events in detail after leaving Beau's Paux. This, too, was characteristic to ease his sense of "not-knowing." Jay told Jon that as he was headed home on Batrie Road it was beginning to rain harder and he lost control of the car and spun out. This was as good as he could muster.

Jay was becoming anxious and scared as he looked up toward Jon. Jon just stood there with a twisted smile on his face, shifting his weight from one leg to the other. He did not know what to do now. Should he reveal the catastrophic events of this early morning to a man clearly out of control emotionally? Jay appeared much like a caged, wounded animal, timid one second exhibiting fear and distrust and the next second, an arrogant, demanding snob who needed no one's assistance. Jon felt helpless in this lonely situation and the tide of many, many days of simpler times flooded him. Absolutely, he thought, "We're both alone now!" Silently Jon sat down beside Jay. Both men sat motionless in a moment of solitude. After what seemed an eternity, Jon's thoughts drifted to earlier times, both good and not so good. He remembered the freedoms that they had experienced and the "aliveness" of it but now it seemed so empty. Jay attempted to light another cigarette in the silence between these two best friends. Still no one spoke a word. Jay didn't know what to say at this point. He really wanted Jon to leave and paradoxically he wanted him to stay. Jay, unconsciously utilizing his sophisticated defense system, thought of his first car and of the friendship that had developed over many years with Jon:

Jay rumbled around within the deep recesses of his mind to reduce the stress and pressure of the present moment. Jon sat silently, each man within his own thoughts.

The day had approached when he could now ask his father to help him buy that red car at the local Ford dealership. Each time in the past when he "needed" something from his family, it became an ordeal for him. He recalled the bicycle incident when he was ten years old. He was the only boy on Lacy Street with no bicycle. For him the possession of a shiny red and white Schwinn with front handlebar brakes was a "status symbol." Even now, "things" were becoming more important than people and relationships. He "needed" things to feel good and little did he know how this seemingly insignificant event was casting his very character and attitude toward life. His father was just beginning his law practice and the answer was always, "We can't afford it yet" or wait until next month." His patience for putting off gratification was nil. He wanted the bicycle now, tomorrow or next month. He would agonize over his self-defined poverty and well; maybe his father didn't really want him to have the bicycle. Other boys had bikes, why couldn't he? Finally in desperation and loss of patience, his father gave into Jay's incessant demands and bought the bicycle for him. It was not the joyous occasion that he had expected. He felt that he was forced to beg for the bike and that intruded negatively into his self-esteem and for the first time, he felt shame. Again now, he wanted something from his father and the past haunted him and the more he ruminated about it, the worse he felt. However, with his driver's education certificate in hand and with a hopeful spirit, he waited anxiously until his father drove into the driveway leading to the house. There was no reason why his request would not be honored but he immediately began to formulate reasons why he "needed" that car. School would be over very soon for another year and since college was on the horizon, he could get a job and help with the expenses. The son of an attorney really didn't need to have an excuse for getting the car, he also reasoned. Money for the car would be no problem he stated adamantly. He deserved to have that car because he had studied hard.

As his Dad rounded the driveway leading to the garage where he had been waiting, he immediately felt a sense of uneasiness regarding the request he would be asking of his father. Nevertheless the time had come and this could not be put off. His father walked toward Jay with a smile on his face, offering an easy access for the onslaught. Before Jay could say anything, his father spoke. Jay, his father began, I suppose it is time we had a talk about the car situation. It is beginning to be inconvenient for me to loan you my car or your Mom's. We need to see about buying a good second-hand car for you. This thrilled Jay to the heights of his being, but he could not allow these feelings to surface and he just simply said, "You're right." Mr. Bienville, an exceptionally caring and sensitive man, (a trait not recognized by Jay) had seen the request coming for the car for quite some time now. All of the negatives that could have arisen did not arise and

Jay felt strangely disappointed! At any rate, the car was in the bag and he was happy about that. He had won again without any effort on his part. Now the searching for the right car would begin and the thought of steering his father to the Ford dealership to look at the one he wanted became Jay's primary concern. Further discussions formulated a plan of attack with a firm agreement to visit various dealerships in the area looking for "the car."

So far, so good Jay mused contentedly. Jay could barely contain his excitement and forthrightly ran to the telephone to present the good news to Kayce (his true love). She would be excited also, he ventured. He would tell her all the details including the scheme for the car he wanted. Of course, there was one more person with whom to share this good news: His best friend, Jonathan Moreau. He and Jonathan had been best friends since the third grade. Jonathan and his family had moved to LaPorte, Louisiana from Dalton, Georgia and he and Jay were friends from the very beginning. Jay found something strangely intriguing about Jonathan, especially his easy going and open manner. They had remained true friends throughout many ordeals and as childhood playmates had been inseparable. Jonathan was not as tall as Jay. He was about 5'11" and had the typical athletic build, broad of shoulder and slim hipped. Jon was sandy haired and had a ruddy complexion. His blue eyes and wide smile were his best features. They were open and friendly. Jay was absolutely ecstatic when he shared the good news with Jon about getting his first car. Jon wanted all the details and Jay was more than happy to oblige. They sat down under the gazebo in the backyard. Jon's eyes sparkled as Jay recounted the events leading up to the decision to purchase the car. Jay did not include the fact that his father was first to propose the purchase of the car with no persuasion on his part. Jay made it sound like a real battle ensued and he had won it single-handedly. They both would now begin to experience the freedom that a "set of wheels" could provide them and the girls also. They both giggled like small children. The idea of responsibility and stewardship never entered into this initial discussion. That would come much later. With this good news both rejoiced in their good fortunes that day; Jay, in getting his first car and Jon, in having Jay as a best friend." Jay's thoughts subsided as he looked over at his very best friend and touched his hand. That was all that was needed. Both men cried as one soul touched the soul of another in desperate pain. An outpouring of stored feelings rushed forth and Jay then was able to tell Jon just how much his friendship had meant to him over the years. Jon sat and listened to his friend.

After the long discussion with Jon, Jay became quiet and somewhat subdued. "Now is the time to tell Jay about what had happened last night," Jon said to himself.

"Jay, I have something very important to tell you and I want you to listen; will you do that for me?" Jay nodded in agreement. Jon slowly revealed the events of the accident and Jay retreated further into his defense system; then as quickly the "no, no, no, no, came from his lips:

A sorrowful sound of someone in deep, agonizing pain gushed from Jay's lips. "Where is Kayce?" shouted Jay, who was a truly desperate man being suddenly set adrift without his anchor to life. "Kayce is at home, I suppose," Jon said. It was a weary and contrite man who looked up at Jon. "Will you bring her to me, Jon? I really need her now."

Jon looked at Jay. He stifled the anger he felt rising and agreed to get Kayce. He left the jail, got his car and slowly started toward Jay and Kayce's home. Yeah, he thought, when things are tough it's Kayce you yell for, but when it's fun and laughter and bawdy sex you want, Shelby's the ticket. Well, Jay, I think you are about to grow up and it ain't gonna be an easy trip. Now, how in the hell am I supposed to break this sorta thing to Kayce?

Chapter 3 – The Wife's Dilemma

Kayce looked out the window again with increasing frustration and anger. Dammit, where was he? Not that it made any difference about the cookout. She had already lied to Val about it. Kayce wondered when lying had become so easy for her. She never had a problem with the truth before; before her life with Jay, that is. In the last nine years she had lied about his drinking behavior so many times. Now it seemed the natural, the right thing to do. Wasn't a wife supposed to stand behind her husband? Besides, Jay was a respected City Attorney. It wouldn't look good if people knew. To Kayce, appearance was very important. But dammit, she was tired of this game, tired of the excuses and lies. She was thirty-three years old. She wanted a baby but who in their right mind would bring a baby into the hell she and Jay called marriage?

As she looked out the window for the fourth time, she wondered out loud, where was he? Of course, it was not unusual that he was late again. What bar did he stop at today? A well-developed sixth sense told her that today was different, somehow their lives were changing and, for some unknown reason, she was frightened. Lord, at thirty-three, she felt old. Kayce had not always been focused. She had been very young when she married the first time. Richard was older and seemed like the perfect "catch" for a young girl not yet eighteen. Besides, he was going to take her out of the hated southern bayou and she would be living in Boston! She thought it would be wonderful but didn't take into account that his family would not ever accept her. Indeed, they seemed to hold a great deal of resentment toward her. Then Rich's affair occurred which sent her flying back to Louisiana. He eventually followed her and there came another affair and her affair in return. The whole thing was nasty and by the time of her divorce, she vowed she would not marry again. Kayce had believed marriage was forever. She had always scorned the men and women who engaged in extramarital relationships. It wasn't so much that she couldn't forgive Richard but found it impossible to forgive herself for her unfaithfulness. Who seduced whom? And why, even now, did the whole thing seem "clean?" She knew Paul had fallen in love with her. She needed him and had felt affection for him. But love him? No, she honestly couldn't say that she loved him. For her, the attraction was purely and simply physical. And fun, lord yes, they did have fun. Kayce had full love of life and living. Looking back, this is what attracted her to Jay. At first, Jay gave the illusion of always having fun with life. Only after they were married did she realize there was very little fun in Jay's life and there were devils that tormented him. Living with Jay was like living with three different men: Not knowing which one would surface each day was the scary part.

Glancing at her watch, she sighed. Which one would come in the house today? The smiling, beguiling boy who would tease her into forgiveness, the moody, sulking despondent who would simply ignore her and stare into some unknown place she would never know or would it be the raging, cruel creature who would most surely verbally abuse her and likely physically hurt her too. She must surely be crazy to stay with him. Yet, leaving him seemed impossible. Kayce let her thoughts take her back to the first time she saw Jay. He was visiting the LeBrochs who lived next door to her parents. He was on their veranda with Maurice, the LeBrochs' middle son. When Kayce saw Jay, she thought he was the most beautiful person she had ever seen. Jacques Bienville was a typical Cajun being tall, olive skinned and dark flashing eyes. Why he did not choose "Jay" rather than "Jack," she did not know nor did she care. He could have called himself Rover and she would have fallen in love with him anyway. Kayce McClary was eleven at the time although she looked sixteen. Kayce was as fair as Jay was dark. Her red-gold hair and bottle green eyes spoke plainly of her Irish/Scottish heritage. She was piss and vinegar and her temper had gotten her in more trouble in her eleven years than most people experience in their whole youth. At eleven, she knew what she wanted and that was Jay Bienville. Kayce began to make her plans, which were a mixture of childish dreams and womanly fantasies.

The soft chimes of the telephone brought Kayce out of a lovely dream. Finally, pushing the last curtain of sleep from her mind, she stumbled to the phone. "Hello, Kayce, this is Suzette." Kayce responded, "Yeah." "Sorry to wake you at this hour." Kayce struggled to see the clock and realized it was still dark outside. She focused on the clock on the desk, good lord, did it say 5:00 A.M.? Suzette continued. Her brother-in-law had just called. Suzette's sister, Monique, had not made it home. Monique was a Registered Nurse at the hospital and had worked an extended shift but had told Philip that she would be home by three. "Kayce, there has been a bad accident on Old Batrie Road which was Monique's back way home." Suzette was frantic. Kayce knew that Batrie Road had some pretty sleazy "clubs." She should know because she suspected that Jay was sleeping with one of the waitresses that worked at Budde's, the most infamous club on that strip. It was rumored that you could buy more than liquor there! God, she hoped that Jay wasn't doing cocaine. Suzette's hysteria brought Kayce out of her thoughts. Kayce told her not to panic, that Monique was probably ok and would be home soon. When Suzette hung up, Kayce said a Hail Mary and prayed that Monique was all right.

As much as Kayce hated confrontations, she vowed that she and Jay would talk about his drinking. What was the name of that place she called once when Jay was drunk and slapped her around? West bay, no, WesterBrook. They seemed understanding and told Kayce that Jay was an Alcoholic! Jay being an alcoholic was so foreign to her. Kayce wanted to run away. She had begun to experience some of those old feelings she had felt when she first became attracted to Paul. Suddenly his smiling face filled her memory. Kayce longed to pick up the phone and call him. She knew, that even after all these years, Paul would respond to her call. She lay her head down on the desk and sobbed softly. Paul was too nice, too kind to be drawn into the dark pit of her life. Kayce knew she would not call him. For some reason Kayce thought of Jon. Jonathan Moreau was Jay's best friend and had been since they were children. Jon was always considerate of Kayce and she always felt safe in his presence. It was Jon she asked about Jay and Shelby. Jon was quick to tell her that Jay loved her but he never denied that Jay and Shelby were having an affair. Kayce had known Shelby ever since they were in elementary school. Shelby was two years older than Kayce and was the talk of Our Lady of Wisdom Catholic School. Kayce was amazed how Shelby could make her uniform look different than the rest of the girls'. She once overheard two of Shelby's boyfriends say that she "put out" and was a "good lay." When Kayce asked her Mother what that meant, Mrs. McClary promptly slapped her across the mouth and said "I'll not be telling you that trash and, Kayce McClary, I better not be hearin' you talking it either!" And, you stay away from that Shelby. She ain't nothin' but trouble and trash!

Kayce shook herself out of the past and looked at the clock. It was 7:00 A.M. As she walked across the den, she caught sight of herself in the mirrored wall around the fireplace. At thirty three, Kayce still looked like a girl. A sad girl with shadows underneath her eyes and stress lines at her mouth but she did not look her years. At five feet five, she could not be called tall but her long legs gave her the appearance of being taller. Her complexion was peaches and cream with a sprinkling of golden freckles. Once she had lamented the freckles but Jon put her mind at rest by saying she looked as if she had been dusted with fairy dust. Her red hair and green eyes were startling but her smile was devastating. It always seemed to hold a secret. It seemed to say "There is more to me than meets the eye, are you willing to take the time to find out what it is? You won't be disappointed." Her figure was drop dead gorgeous. You really couldn't call her beautiful but she definitely had presence.

Kayce Bienville did not enter a room unnoticed. She had a quality that immediately captivated every man in the room. The women were at a loss to understand it and as much as they hated to admit it, they too were drawn to her and liked Kayce. Not only that, they trusted her. If you had a secret, Kayce would keep it. Kayce made a face at the woman in the mirror and started to the kitchen to make coffee. Just as it began to perk, the doorbell sounded.

Whoever was there was an impatient jerk. As she entered the foyer she heard Jon's voice, "Kayce, answer the door. Kace are you awake? Kaaaacey answer the door." "Dammit Jon, pipe down. Do you want to wake everyone on the block? Come in. Oh lord, Jon, its Jay isn't?" Jon looked at her pale face. "Yes Kace, but let's get to the kitchen and don't drop out on me. Jay's not hurt but he is in jail." Kayce's concern turned to anger. "I'll bet it has to do with his late visits at the Paux or more likely at Buddes. Serves him right and it won't hurt him to cool his heels in there for a few hours, Jon." "Yes Kayce, it does have something to do with his drinking but I'm afraid it is serious enough that a few hours won't take care of it. There was an accident on the old Batrie Road and a nurse was badly injured. How she is going to fare, no one knows. Jay was driving the other car. It doesn't look good for him, Kayce. He is asking for you." Kayce slowly arose out of her chair. "Let me get showered and dressed. I'll only be a few minutes." As she left the kitchen, Jon looked around and decided to fix her breakfast. He knew French toast was her favorite so he immediately began frying the bacon and making the toast. He was setting the table when she appeared. In spite of the strain showing on her face, he thought she was the loveliest woman he had ever seen. She smiled as she noticed that Jon had made her favorite breakfast. How like him to remember. She forced herself to eat and thanked Jon. They cleared the table, loaded the dishwasher and left the house. As they drove to the jail Kayce dreaded the day ahead of her. She didn't know what to expect but knew whatever it turned out to be, it wasn't going to be pleasant.

As Jon turned into the parking lot, he reached over and took her hand. "We will get through this Kace, you'll see." She squeezed his hand and together they walked into the jail. The bailiff announced to Jay that he had visitors. Jon relinquished Kayce to Jay and left. He didn't want to be present for their discussion. He heard Jay say "we're in pretty deep trouble this time Kayce." Jon shook his head. Jay actually believed that Kayce could fix this for him. He heard Kayce reply. "Jay, I'll stand by you and I'll help you all I can. But, I can't lie for you, not anymore. There has to be some help out there somewhere. And you've got to find it. I can't do it for you." Jon was flabbergasted. Well, Kayce seemed to be wising up. Wonder where this came from? Kayce's words were like a dash of ice water to Jay's present feelings. He dropped his head into his cupped hands and lamented, "God, Now Kayce is turning her back on me!" This was almost more than he could bear. Kayce reached over and placed her arm around his shoulders. "Jay, forgive my abruptness. Damn, I'm worried about you. It's just I'm afraid that this time it's a bit much and a lot of it. You are going to have to do for yourself. This drinking thing is way out of hand but now is not the time for us to get into that. You've got too much to handle now that is immediate. I've already begun to inquire about bail. I'm not sure how that stands. Since I know Suzette, I'll check on Monique through her." Jay looked at Kayce with horror in his eyes, "not Monique, not the mother of those three little babies." He grabbed Kayce and cried. Kayce gently rocked him in her arms. "Jay, sweet, please try to sleep. You can't do anything right now and it won't help anyone to keep this self-torment up. I've got to go now but I'll be back. Please try to rest." She kissed him gently and sat with him until he fell into a fitful sleep. Quietly she left the jail cell after calling to the attendant. Jon heard Kayce's footsteps coming down the long hallway from the jail cell. He met her at the door and together they walked out to her car.

Chapter 4 – Wheels of Justice

The wheels of justice grind slowly. The State's assault case was dismissed because of a legal technical error. Some people spoke actively of a "white-wash" job of the case and no one seemed interested in pursuing it. However, the judge presiding over the proceedings was highly displeased with Jay Bienville. The Civil suit filed against him by the accident victim was scheduled to begin this morning and Jay was "anxious" about it.

Jay still could not believe he was in a courtroom as a defendant and that he was being tried in a civil court for vehicular assault with personal injury. There had been an ongoing stream of witnesses and Jay realized for the first time that being on the other side of the table was a helluva lot harder than the side he was accustomed to occupying.

He turned his thoughts back to Shelby, who was on the stand. She had been asked many questions and was looking rather confused at this point. The plaintiff's attorney was asking her why she would have served alcohol to a person who was obviously already intoxicated. Jay's attorney, Walton Pierce, quickly got to his feet and voiced a strong objection to that line of questioning. "Your Honor, my client has not been charged with any offense related to alcohol use." "But Your Honor," Jean Johnson (Monique's attorney) retorted, "this line of questioning has relevance in this case." The Judge quickly commanded, "Both of you to my chambers, now!" Judge Holloway excused Shelby from the stand, "You may step down but the right to recall you will be honored by this Court." The Judge calmly called a ten-minute recess and the Judge and both attorneys quietly left the courtroom. Jay did not look at Shelby nor turn his head. He continued to look straight ahead as if deep in thought.

Judge Holloway sat down at his desk prepared for an argument over the matter of judicial prudence. Jay's attorney pointed out the potential of an argument for a mis-trial because of the inappropriate enthusiastic remarks made by Ms Johnson, the Plaintiff's attorney. Jean sat quietly allowing the defense attorney to present his side of the argument. "This man has not been charged with a citation for any offense involving alcohol. This case before the Court deals with assault of another person via the use of an automobile. The decision handed down by the Court is statutorily obliged to consider only the facts regarding the accident." Jay's attorney's attacking manner quickly crumbled as he realized what he had just said. The Judge looked at him and calmly said, "Yall ready to go back and resolve this matter?" Both agreed.

Monique's attorney had a smirk on her face as she returned to the courtroom. Walton Pierce had learned another valuable lesson: "Don't give more than is necessary to win your point!"

The Judge and both attorneys re-entered the courtroom and the Court was called to order by the bailiff. The Judge then gave a response to the objection made by Jay's attorney, "Sustained, and recall Shelby Longmire to the stand." Shelby took the witness chair and the bailiff reminded her she was still under oath. Monique's attorney, now more confident than ever and rather forcefully, stated, "You served alcoholic beverages to a man who was obliviously intoxicated?" "Objection Your Honor," Jay's attorney responded; "that calls for a conclusion by the witness." Over-ruled," the Judge snapped back, glaring at both attorneys, "please, re-phrase your question." Jean began again, "Ms. Longmire, you are a waitress at Budde's, correct?" "Yes, I am," she responded almost hesitantly. "When you served the drink to the defendant, what was his attitude toward you?" Shelby knew where the line of questioning was leading and finally in her exhaustion and utter emotional confusion, exploded! "Why would you ask me such a thing? Do you think I would deliberately do anything to hurt Jay Bienville? Never!! He is the father of my child! Do you think I would want him hurt?

Kayce was listening to Shelby's testimony. Jon went unobserved as he watched Kayce. He didn't think she could look any paler than she already looked but as Shelby made her announcement about her daughter, Marianne, Kayce jumped to her feet and her pallor increased. Jon reached her as she slumped to the floor. Jay was so intent on Shelby's testimony that he did not see Kayce leap to her feet. Indeed, he was unaware of her until the commotion in the back of the courtroom caused him to turn around. He saw Jon and another man lift her from the floor and carry her out of the room. Both attorneys were startled by the events in the rear of the courtroom.

Jay's attorney requested a recess until 1:00 P.M. because it was approaching lunch anyway. The Judge granted the request until 1:00 P.M. and adjourned the proceedings and dismissed the jury.

After lunch Court was reconvened promptly at 1:00 P.M. The jury was brought back to the courtroom and the court was called to order by the bailiff as Judge Holloway entered and took his seat.

Judge Holloway again recalled Shelby Longmire to the stand. "Your witness, Ms. Johnson," he said with little energy in his voice. "Now, Ms. Longmire, let us get through this question once and for all. You have testified under oath that you served drinks to the defendant, Mr. Bienville. Is that correct? "Yes, that is correct," Shelby responded slowly. "Had he been drinking prior to entering Budde's," Monique's attorney said, her voice getting more dramatic and building. Shelby looked toward the Judge and he indicated that she should answer the question, yes or no.

"Yes, he had been drinking," she said in a much-subdued tone. "I want you to listen carefully to this question, Ms. Longmire. Would you have felt it safe to allow your daughter to ride in the car with Mr. Bienville when he left Budde's?" Jay's attorney sat motionless. He knew the consequences when she answered and he knew the answer as well as anyone in the courtroom. Shelby again looked at the Judge and then toward Jay. "Answer the question, Ms. Longmire," the Judge directed. Finally she responded, "No," in an almost inaudible voice. Would you repeat your answer, please?" "No," she said. No further questions Your Honor." "Any redirect," he said toward Jay's attorney. "No, Your Honor." "You may step down, Ms. Longmire," the Judge said with a measure of relief. A twinge of legal consciousness intruded but he dismissed it as calmly as he had just dismissed the witness. He had been drinking prior to the accident and this witness had just confirmed that fact. It was 3:30 P.M. and the Judge made a decision to call an adjournment for the day. Court is adjourned and will re-convene at 8:00 tomorrow morning and, members of the jury, let me remind you that all facts pertinent to this case have not been presented and no discussing this case outside this court room. Do you understand what I'm saying?" They nodded in unison an affirmative answer and filed out of the courtroom.

Jay and his attorney walked out of the courthouse toward his car. Jay remarked to his attorney that things didn't look too good for him now. Walton Pierce said simply that he would try to mitigate the damages and proceed from there. "I'll meet you here at 8:00 A.M.," he said as Jay switched on the ignition. "O.K." and Jay drove toward the hospital to check on Kayce.

Kayce awoke in All Saints General Hospital. It was Jon sitting beside her bed, not Jay. Suddenly, recollection of everything, the accident, arrest, trial and Shelby's terrible revelation washed over her. Kayce felt the terrible retching begin and she vomited for what seemed to her, to be hours. Jon bathed her face and gently pressed her back onto the hospital bed. He had called for a nurse who appeared with an injection for her. Kayce felt the sting of the needle and slipped into welcomed oblivion.

Jon walked out of the hospital into the warm sunshine. Where would all of this end? What was Shelby's disclosure going to do to Jay and Kayce's marriage? Jon knew that Jay had been supporting Marianne and was not opposed. It was obvious that Marianne was Jay's daughter. She had his coloring, build and mannerisms. Jon had tried to get Jay to confess everything to Kayce. He knew it was only a matter of time before she found out. Frankly, Marianne had her third birthday six months ago. That Jay had been able to keep it from Kayce this long was amazing. Each time Jon mentioned telling Kayce the truth, Jay would simply laugh. He said, "Kayce was for loving but Shelby was for other things" and that Kayce did not need to know anything about her. Jon was at a loss to understand Jay's attitude about the whole thing. He felt it had to do with Jay's drinking. No man in his right mind would have put Kayce aside for any woman. Jon had a secret only he and God knew and that was Jon's deep love for Kayce. In his nighttime fantasy, Jon would sweep Kayce away and make love to her the way she should be loved. Jon shook these thoughts out of his mind. This kind of thinking was dangerous, very dangerous. He knew Jay had a bad temper and if he knew about this, he would explode. He could not discuss with Jay, ever! Jon strode across the street to a pay telephone. He needed to call Budde's; he needed to talk with Shelby. After adjournment, Shelby had gone back to Budde's. That dammed attorney had tricked her. She had confessed that Jay was Marianne's father to the whole frigging town of LaPorte! If she lived to be one hundred, she would never forget Kayce Bienville's face as she bolted up from her seat. Shelby had nothing against Kayce, as a matter fact, Shelby sorta admired Kayce. She genuinely regretted that Kayce had been hurt. Lord, if looks could kill, Shelby knew she would be dead at this moment. Jon had literally stopped her testimony cold when he shot her the death look from the rear of the courtroom. She and Jon never got along too well but since both loved Jay, they practiced armed neutrality and managed to be civil to each other. Shelby looked up as the bartender called her to the phone. She crushed out her cigarette and strode over to answer the phone.

"Shelby, this is Jon." "Dear lord, Shelby thought, here it comes!" "Yeah Jon, I know I screwed up real bad today but please save your lecture for another time, I've had about as much as I can take today." Jon smiled bitterly to himself. It was just like Shelby to be concerned only for herself. In this area, she and Jay were exactly alike. "No Shelby, it is much too late for lectures," he said. "Kayce is in the hospital. You and Jay are responsible for her being there. Jay can't go to her to explain and so you've got to. I don't know if Kayce will listen to you but you must try. Shelby, you know that no matter what Jay feels for you, he loves Kayce and unless she ends it, he will stay married to her. You've got to try to bridge the gap. Not for you and Jay. At this moment I don't give a rat's ass what happens to either of you but your selfish actions has hurt two innocent people. Kayce and Marianne deserve better. Marianne deserves to know her Father and if you don't do something, she will never get the chance. Jay Bienville won't sacrifice Kayce for anyone, not even his child. I know it and so do you! Kayce is the key. You must make it work." Shelby had listened to Jon without saying anything. When he finished, she thought for a minute. He was right. She would have to try. Quietly Shelby said, "Yes Jon. Believe it or not, I do love my daughter and want to make things right for her. Bye Jon." Jon hung up without answering her.

When Jay entered All Saints Hospital he was greeted with curious stares. The hospital staff was aware of the drama that took place at the courthouse earlier. Jay chose to ignore those rude people and demanded to see Kayce. After Kayce's physician intervened, Jay was shown to his wife's room. As he entered the room he saw that she was asleep. Looking down at her, Jay felt an unfamiliar feeling and he was surprised when he identified it as "fear." He wasn't exactly sure what he was afraid of but he was scared. He couldn't admit he was afraid of losing her so he pushed this uncomfortable feeling aside. Gently he took her hand. At his touch, her eyes opened. She gave him a weak smile and told him to go home. "Jay I just can't talk now, I can't make any decisions now and it just wouldn't be right. And forgive me, but I don't want to see you right now." Softly Jay said, "O.K." and got up to leave. At the door, he turned and said, "I love you, Kayce." Kayce looked at him through her sedation, "I know," she said.

When court was re-convened at 8:00 A.M., Jay's attorney made a request to the Judge to approach the bench. The Judge granted the request. "Your Honor, may we meet in your chambers?" The Judge was in a rather foul mood and he refused the request and offered no reason for the refusal. He waved both attorneys to come forward. He leaned forward and said, "What is it now?" "Your Honor, Ms. Johnson and I met last night and we discussed this case in detail and we are ready to make a plea but under extenuating circumstances. We are prepared to concede to the accident and the ensuing physical injuries inflicted upon the plaintiff. Further, the defendant has agreed to pay all hospital and Physician expenses associated with said accident plus compensatory damages amounting to six months' salary while she recuperates at home and reasonable attorney fees. Part of this plead is predicated upon my client not being formally charged or arrested until seventy-two hours after the accident. Hallman Vs Smith, AL, 1983, set the precedence for my motion. We also desire to mitigate court expense and the court's time, Your Honor." "I am aware of that widely publicized case and there is a commonality in this present case. I will call a recess for one hour and I'll then render a decision on your motion." Court was then adjourned for one hour by the bailiff.

Monique's attorney had listened carefully to Jay's attorney's proposal. Of course, her main concern was taking care of her client's needs and could not fault the offer that was being submitted for the court's consideration. But Jean Johnson and Jay had been classmates in law school and she had admired his quick mind and easy grasp of the intricate principles of law. Recently she had observed his expertise in the courtroom. Unfortunately, she also knew of his late nights at Budde's and other indiscretions that were whispered among the legal community. Jay's father was a force to be reckoned with and so no one openly remarked on Jay's, often times, erratic behavior. Jean's mind frantically searched for a way to make this terrible incident benefit Jay; i.e., to turn him around or at least to make him look at where his life was heading. Jean prayed for insight and found herself accepting the offer but with two additional conditions: (1. Jay would agree to a psychiatric evaluation, and (2). Jay would provide "pro bono" legal work (at least forty hours) for victims of accidents involved in alcohol-related accidents.

One hour had elapsed and exactly on time, the bailiff reconvened the court.

Judge Holloway made a general statement to the open court and then specifically charged the jury with the motion as presented by the defense attorney. He explained that both attorneys had reached a general consensus regarding the disposition of the case and their further services would not be required and subsequently he dismissed them and thanked them.

He then turned his attention to the two attorneys standing in front of him. "I have made the decision to accept the conditions as set forth in your original motion." Jean Johnson then interrupted, "Your Honor, I require two additional conditions," and she proceeded to explain. To her amazement the Judge didn't chastise her for her legal impropriety. Both the Judge and the defense attorney nodded in complete agreement. The Judge then motioned for Jay to stand. "You have heard the agreement reached by this Court. Do you have any questions or direct comments before I enter the order?" Jay almost meekly replied, "No, Your Honor." "So ordered and this court is adjourned and case closed," the Judge said as his gavel fell hard. As Jean walked out of the courtroom she said a short prayer of thanks.

It was three weeks before Shelby mustered the nerve to face Kayce. She dressed carefully and wore a navy skirt of reasonable length and a white blouse trimmed in lace. Her conservative white pumps completed the picture. No doubt, Shelby still looked sensual but it was somewhat subdued. Her makeup was still a little heavy but Shelby had noticed some lines and other evidences of her strenuous nightlife beginning to show on her face. Shelby swore silently, what the hell, I'm what I am and it is too late to change it now. Marianne skipped into the room. Immediately Shelby's demeanor changed. It softened and, unknown to her, some of the years' toll had vanished. It was evident that Marianne was the love of Shelby's life. She had dressed her carefully for the meeting with her stepmother. It was imperative that Kayce like the child. Marianne looked like a dark angel. Her black hair was pulled back and braided in one long braid which was held at the top of her head by a gold barrette (her third birthday gift from her Father). The pale pink dress reached just above her chubby knees, which were covered with white lace stockings, which ended at her dainty feet shod in white patent leather shoes. She wore small gold studs in her ears. Her black eyes were framed with gold-tipped lashes and her rosebud mouth was perfect.

Shelby thought, no one could see this child and not love her! She gathered up Marianne and said a silent prayer that she would be on her best behavior and loaded her into the car. As they drove to Jay's home, it dawned on Shelby that she had never been there before. Of all the years she had been in Jay's life, she had never been invited to his home. Bitterly, she admitted to herself "a man's mistress is never invited to social gatherings of friends and family." For the first time, she felt some shame and regret about her relationship with Jay. She had wanted with him what he had with Kayce. Today, she realized that it would never be. The most she could hope for was acceptance of Marianne by the Bienville family. And, as Jon had so plainly put it, that was up to Kayce. As she turned onto the drive, she drew in her breath, parked the car, extracted Marianne from the car seat and purposefully walked up to the door.

At the door chime, Kayce appeared. If Shelby's appearance startled her, she gave no notice of it. Good breeding surfaced, and Kayce invited the two of them in. Such beautiful furniture, Shelby sighed. She prayed silently: Please, please, Marianne, don't break anything! Shelby saw that Kayce was studying Marianne and had the good sense not to say anything. Abruptly, Kayce called for Beatrice, and a middle-aged woman in crisp black and white appeared. "Bea, I believe this lovely young lady is named Marianne, her Mother and I have a few things to discuss which probably will bore her. Why don't you take her to the kitchen for milk and cookies, then to the storage house to see the new kittens? Oh yes, we don't want to soil her dress, so see if you can arrange an apron to protect it." Kayce turned her beautiful smile to Marianne and said "How would you like that?" Marianne clapped her hands in delight, "May I Mamma?" Shelby nodded and Marianne turned to Bea and held out her hand. "Do you really have kittens?" Bea laughed, "we surely do, missy." Marianne turned quickly and ran back in front of Kayce. "Thank you, Mrs. Bienville," Kayce reached out and touched the child's cheek. "You are welcome my dear, now run along with Bea, we'll join you in a little while." After the two had left, Kayce turned her attention to Shelby. Kayce appraised the other woman. Shelby's lifestyle showed but she was still lovely. Kayce thought, "She looks like a Barbie doll that has been played with too much and too hard." Kayce's sensitive nature surfaced and momentarily, she felt pity for the woman across from her but, also, to her surprise, a grudging respect. It took guts to come to this house. Kayce realized it was for Marianne's sake and no other reason.

Kayce said "Shelby, let's not insult each other with false feelings and reasons. You are here because of Marianne and I understand that. I am not asking you to explain or apologize for your affair with Jay. You may be surprised to know, I credit most of the responsibility for the thing to Jay. Of course, you could have refused but he shouldn't have pursued you, not after we were married that is. So, let's get past the "blame" thing and get on with why you are here. Shelby, leaned back in the chair, this lady has class, she thought. "Kayce, my concern is that you will make it difficult for Marianne to know her Father. As a matter fact, I didn't give her Jay's last name because I was afraid it would hurt him, professionally, you know? He said it would and I believed him. He has been a great financial father but has spent very little time with her. She knows he is her Daddy but really doesn't know him. He probably has seen her six or seven times in the last three years. She is reaching the age of questions. Quite frankly, I don't know what to tell her." To her dismay, her voice broke, and Shelby said: "Kayce, I don't want her to be like me. Don't get me wrong; I'm not apologizing for my life. I've lived it as I pleased. I just want better for my little girl. That's natural isn't it, to want better for your child?" Kayce had listened without interrupting. Now she spoke. "Yes, Shelby, it is perfectly natural for a parent to want better for her child. And, I have no fault with you for that. You have nothing to worry about from me. Jay and I will have to discuss this when we get through this ordeal. But, I assure you, I will never stand in the way of his having a relationship with his daughter. As far as I am concerned, Marianne is welcome here. I hope you know that Marianne will never be treated with anything but kindness from me." Shelby knew Kayce spoke the truth. She had seen the gentleness in Kayce's eyes and touch when Marianne thanked her for allowing the visit with the kittens. Kayce stood and said "Now, let's see if we can find Bea and Marianne." As they approached the storage room, they heard Marianne say, "I want the yellow one with the white socks." Kayce looked quizzingly at Shelby who smiled and nodded an affirmative. Back at the house, Bea helped Marianne find a basket to take "Mittens" home in and Kayce and Shelby had coffee. As Shelby, Marianne and "Mittens" drove away, Bea put her arm around Kayce. "You are one unusual lady, Kayce." Her green eyes were sparkling with tears, "Yes Bea, I think I covered my desire to scratch her eyes out quite well!" Bea laughed softly and led Kayce back into the house.

As she drove back to her apartment, Shelby was thinking: This went better than expected. True enough, she and Kayce would never be fast friends but they would be able to maintain a civil relationship because of Marianne. Now, the problem was Jay. Shelby was beginning to see Jay in a different light. Their relationship was over. She felt a bit sad but strangely enough, a sense of relief was there too. It was as if she had closed the door on a less than happy event and was ready for a new beginning. She and Jay would always have contact because of Marianne but beyond that, it was over. Jay was just going to have to accept it.

Kayce knew the situation with Shelby and Marianne had broken the deep personal bond and love she had felt for Jay. The completely trusting attitude was dead. More than anything else she was angry with Jay, Shelby, and with some misgivings, she harbored secret resentments toward that lovely child, Marianne also. The thoughts of the past year only served to fuel the feelings Kayce was experiencing. In a burst of emerging frustration and despair, Kayce exploded! Someone has to do something! I can't handle this anymore! I must make a decision for us both, she thought. Kayce finally made the decision to call WesterBrook again. Once before she had called them but this time it would be different. Jay would be admitted for treatment this time. The receptionist answered after the third ring and Kayce requested the admission office extension. The benefits clerk answered.

Kayce was scared. She timidly requested information regarding getting someone admitted to the hospital. The clerk was kind, considerate, and helpful. Insurance information was gathered and an appointment was scheduled for a pre-admission assessment. The clerk asked Kayce, "Do you think your husband will keep this appointment?" Kayce was quick to assure the clerk that Jay would be on time for the assessment. Additionally, she was given the benefits information she had requested. Jay's insurance carrier would pay for the treatment in full. That cost included full medical detoxification services, rehabilitation, and up to two years of continuing care services. This sounded fine to Kayce and she told the clerk to expect Jay at the appointed hour. Kayce hung up the telephone and began to second-guess what she had done. Yes, Jay needed treatment for something but what? Was he "crazy" or was he, indeed, an alcoholic! Next, telling Jay about what she had done! What would he do? How would he react to this? He had defended several clients who drank more than he did. He had voiced great contempt for the majority of them and mostly told jokes about "those crazies." She wondered as she wrote the information on a scratch pad. It really didn't matter how he choose to react to this appointment; he would go. Period! Kayce glanced up at the wall clock: Quarter to five. Normally Jay arrived home by 6:30 P.M. and then she would tell him, whether he was drinking or not, friendly or not, angry or not, whatever, she would tell him then.

Chapter 5 - Consultation

Judge Holloway's order for the psychiatric evaluation angered Jay but he also realized that Walton had done his best legal dancing in his defense. He did not know a psychiatrist in LaPorte and it was just as well that he didn't, people were too nosey anyway. He decided to check the yellow pages in New Orleans and the first name he saw was Macklin Devere. He called and made the appointment. The receptionist seemed hurried and cut him off abruptly after scheduling the appointment. The nerve of that "bitch," Jay thought to himself as he hung up the telephone. Today was Tuesday and the appointment was set for Friday morning. Jay decided not to say anything to Kayce about it until after it was over. He would simply tell her he had business in New Orleans that day. Simple enough, he thought.

His appointment with Dr. Macklin Devere, a psychiatrist whose office was located in the quaint and exquisite French quarter of New Orleans, was scheduled for 10:00 A.M. on Friday morning. Just the thought angered him. "You keep this appointment," the City EAP Counselor had said to him. A real demanding attitude, Jay thought. Jay muttered to himself as he walked alone into the "shrink's" outer office and thought to himself that this was not so bad but would he enter the "inner sanctum" when his name was called. That thought concerned him.

He took the chair nearest the door and sat down almost meekly. But he was fuming silently. The receptionist acknowledged him and said, "You're early, and the doctor will see you shortly." She came over to his chair and requested that he complete a personal information sheet. He accepted the form and began to read through it prior to answering the questions. This added inconvenience angered him with an additional invasion of his privacy and, in writing, no less. As Jay sat there smoking his third cigarette, he completed the demographics form given to him by the "cold-natured" woman. He questioned the details requested by the form and with contempt he hurriedly and in a fast scrawling manner finished the chore. And he didn't sign it as requested by the last sentence on the form, only as a final show of arrogance and disdain.

He stood up, walked over to the glass enclosure and flipped the completed form toward the receptionist, releasing the remaining displeasure. The receptionist replied, "Thank you, and the doctor will see you soon." He returned to his chair and lit another cigarette watching the smoke whirl toward the ceiling fan. The statement by the receptionist resulted in his pulse rate jumping and increased perspiration. His hands were now clammy and he kept them dry by rubbing them on his pants. Fifteen minutes passed and he lit another cigarette and tried to disassociate himself from this anxiety-ridden situation.

The past six months swept gushingly into his mind as his eyes reddened ever so slightly. Jay was hurting more than he cared to admit, to anyone or to himself. How could his life decline to such a low? He felt no need to see another person, much less a psychiatrist, about his problems. He was self-reliant and he had to handle this situation himself with no outside help. His "impeccable father" had fostered that notion onto him. However, the city EAP had wanted this consultation and the court was enforcing it. Jay sat with his thoughts of "why me" and his arrogance and excuse making; I've had a run of bad luck, etc. Jay's thoughts of the automobile accident and the severe injury to the young woman continued to be blocked from his consciousness. Even Kayce had gone along with the scheduling of the consultation but she categorically refused to accompany him to the office. "You have to do this alone, Jay!" Again Jay became self-absorbed in his own thoughts and the terrible situation that brought him to this mahogany adorned office.

The telephone rang loudly on the receptionist's desk and his pulse raced even harder. Was it time? Why am I so anxious about meeting with this "shrink?" The receptionist motioned toward the door and Jay slowly got up from the leather chair and walked toward the door. He opened the heavy wooden door and walked inside. Dr. Devere was dressed sporting a gray linen suit, pale pink shirt, and a perfectly matched damask tie. A tiny goatee also adorned his chin. Gold rimmed, round spectacles completed the picture. Dr. Devere met Jay at the door and escorted him into his office. "Come in and have a seat," he said, motioning toward the available chair. Jay felt somewhat timid and shy as he offered his hand. A warm, alive handshake Jay thought to himself. Many thoughts now raced through Jay's mind. Jay was no longer in his domain of courts, briefs, attorneys, juries, and legal books. Now he was on this "psychiatric turf" and he would make the proper adjustments. He "must" make those adjustments, he thought. Jay's own opinions and perceptions regarding the results of this interview were foremost now. He must be clearly in control of this session and exhibit his intellectual ability and display his emotional control to this man.

Dr. Devere took a seat in an overstuffed leather chair and Jay took the one adjacent to it. "A real cozy situation," he mused. Dr. Devere initiated some small talk to help with the anxiety and the emerging defensiveness he recognized in this new patient. He asked Jay if he had any difficulty in locating his office and Jay had remarked dryly and with no affect that he had none. A question of how he was feeling was also met with the same cold response, "I'm feeling about as well as could be expected, considering the circumstances." Dr. Devere's immediate task was now to simply engage Jay by decreasing the emerging levels of anxiety. The psychiatrist recognized clearly that his client needed to understand more about the process if he was to decrease the anxiety and underlying fears that were driving the anxiety. It was tantamount at this particular juncture that he assist Jay to be more at ease.

Dr.Devere began the session thusly: "I have some background material regarding this consultation or assessment, if you prefer, from the City EAP. I want to be sure I get the basic facts straight in my mind. Can you tell me in your own words what led up to this appointment?" Jay felt better almost instantaneously after hearing Dr. Devere's statement.

Jay continued with the account as best he could bringing him back to the present time. "Good," Dr. Devere said. "Let's talk more in depth about your alcohol use, Jay," Dr. Devere cleverly interjected, catching Jay somewhat off guard. Jay then related his history of alcohol use since age 16. At this point, Dr. Devere asked, "Jay, how would you define the problem that brought you here today?" Jay reviewed the alcohol use, the DUI's, the accident, quarrels with Kayce and other family members, and his diminished enthusiasm for his work and play. "I wouldn't know how to state the problem, Dr. Devere," Jay resounded. This remark suggested to Dr. Devere Jay's fear of being misunderstood or of being judged. Dr. Devere also noticed inappropriate affective displays as Jay was explaining the accident and the severe injury to the young woman. He began to get clues leading to a type of amnestic disorder (possibly a "blackout") surrounding the seriousness of the event. Jay's affect changed little as he recounted the tragic accident; as if it happened to someone else; as if he had no recollection of it. Dr.Devere further recognized early on in the session that Jay was trying very hard to present himself in the best possible light and this was hindering the process of assessment. Again, Dr. Devere remarked to Jay, "I think I'm getting a good picture of what's going on but please continue." This again eased Jay's anxiety a little more and he proceeded to explain deeper feelings and hurts, specifically his low self-esteem and his wanting to please everyone. Never had he said that to another living soul and it surprised him how easy it flowed from his lips. Further he told the psychiatrist of his inordinate levels of fear and the underlying anger associated with this visit. His words were gushing forth as never before and Dr. Devere sat and listened attentively. After a while, Jay remarked that he felt physically tired and Dr. Devere stated that he understood how such emotional turmoil could tire him. Dr. Devere knew intuitively that Jay had needed this emotional catharsis. Afterwards, Jay's entire demeanor changed with a corresponding change in his presentation of himself. Jay had originally planned to "con" this man but his plans had gone awry; the release was good for him, he thought. Dr. Devere had already begun to formulate his diagnostic impressions as he listened intently to every spoken word and observed every physical nuance exhibited by Jay. At this point he asked Jay a very pointed question, "Jay, with all of the personal, intimate, and quite tragic details you have provided during this assessment, what do you think needs to be done next?" This statement puzzled Jay. "You're the psychiatrist," he thought to himself.

Jay was reluctant to speak and rather than just stare at the man, he gently lowered his eyes. At this, Dr. Devere moved closer to Jay, touched his hand, and offered him support, and encouragement. He simply said, "Jay, alcoholism is a disease, it is fatal if left untreated, it's progressive, it's chronic, and you need to stop drinking." Jay couldn't disagree with the notion of ceasing his alcohol use, but "the disease?" He didn't know about that! Dr. Devere was being somewhat less directive than usual to allow some of these hard words to sink slowly into Jay's mind. He continued, "Further, I can find no issues dealing with psycho-pathology or any acute psychosis; I did observe some inappropriate affective displays (Jay asked for clarification of that statement and the Doctor willingly obliged) while you were relating the accident and its subsequent events, but no overriding intensities of feelings. There are no typical disturbances of thought processes present but your reactions to life seem to be based on a personal conception of how you perceive the world and how it ought to operate and not upon given facts. Relationships described were of a narcissistic nature; i.e., "a need to live a completely free and detached life." Further, the family dynamics described by you exhibited signs of emotional deprivation, possibly from the paternal side of the family." Jay sat enthralled with what he was hearing. "I also think that you have no clear recollection of all of the events of the accident. The normal levels of anxiety and fear were very apparent initially but you were able to summon the appropriate coping skills to substantially alleviate them. I have not noticed any severe resistance to me and that is a very positive sign for you. Jay, I believe we are in complete agreement regarding all we have discussed today and now I want to know how you plan to use what's happened here today."

"Dr. Devere," Jay began, "I had great difficulties in keeping this appointment. I retreated to an infantile level of maturity and coping: I wanted to just run away. Kayce, my wife of nine years, framed it really nicely for me when she said, "Jay, you have to do this alone!" and that was the existential remark that really motivated me to keep this appointment despite my severe anxieties and fears. I had to! Something is wrong; you know it and I have refused to "know it." I want to really thank you for your kindness, caring, and consideration. The City EAP will want a summary from you, so please do what you must do." With that, Dr. Devere wished Jay well and walked him to the door and through the reception room to the outer door. Jay extended his hand and again thanked Dr. Devere for his time.

Dr. Devere then closed the door behind Jay and returned to his desk to dictate the diagnostic summary. From the history surrounding the scheduling of the appointment, Dr. Devere had decided to immediately utilize the C. A. G. E. Questionnaire (Ewing, 1984) (that included the following:

C – “Cut down”: Has anyone ever recommended that you cut back or stop your use of alcohol?

A – “Annoyed”: Have you ever felt annoyed or angry if someone comments on your drinking?

G – “Guilt’: Have there been times when you’ve felt guilty about or regretted things that occurred because of drinking?

E – “Eye-Opener”: Have you ever used alcohol to help you get started in the morning to steady your nerves? A positive response to three of the four indicated an alcohol problem existed thereby getting to the heart of the assessment rather quickly.

Jay had responded positively to all four questions and that fact strongly indicated the existence of the disease of alcoholism. His full report would be sent to the EAP of the City of LaPorte as soon as it returned from his transcriptionist. He would also send a personal note to Jay.

Jay left New Orleans as rapidly as he could and the thought of getting a drink did not enter his mind. Home to his wife was the one thing on his mind presently. He wanted to tell Kayce of the morning’s events and how he felt about it. The past three weeks had been most difficult for Jay as his neatly created world began to fall down around him. With the accident and the resulting court order because of the severe injury to Monique, coupled with the psychiatric evaluation that would recommend strongly that he seek professional help, Jay had run out of options. Even now the city EAP was heavily involved and that meant he had no way to cover this up or push it under the tug. The events must play themselves out. His job status was tenuous, at best, he surmised and his family was disintegrating before his very eyes. His urge to run away, stay in the bottle, was strong and deep down he knew what he must do. He would discuss this situation with Kayce when he returned home. He would call the City EAP the first thing in the morning. Should he call for an appointment for a consultation at WesterBrook? Oh yes, lovely WesterBrook named after a rather older mountain gentleman and his fortune and "misfortune." Presently Jay's strong convictions sustained his efforts.

Onward he drove toward home rehearsing how he would present this information to Kayce. At this point he could not afford to waiver. This must be done; I can't continue with this life of alcohol use. It must stop! However, the "how" scared him! This notion had occurred to Jay in the past, but it always ended with another bottle and more empty promises to himself and to others. Dr. Devere had told him simply that he had a disease and treatment was available. Dr. Devere stated three pertinent ideas to Jay that stuck with him: (1). Jay had developed tolerance to alcohol (takes more and more to get the desired "buzz"), (2). that he suspected physical dependence with physical withdrawal symptoms (headaches, sleep disturbances, agitation and anxiety coupled with hostility, depression, hyperactivity, hyper-sensitive to noises, nausea with stomach-aches and vomiting, elevated blood pressured, potential for heart palpitations and arrhythmias, to name a few), and (3), an irresistible urge and need for alcohol when it is not readily available. Jay could not disagree as he brought this back to his memory. However, he didn't readily validate Dr. Devere's statement while he was in his office just hours earlier. Jay's mind was still intact and the thought of a statement remembered years earlier surfaced clearly: "Drunkenness is nothing but a condition of insanity purposely assumed!" Was he a moral degenerate who had purposely chosen to feel the way he now felt? And through a "lack of will and emotional immaturity" allowed himself to lose his self-respect, the respect of his family and friends, and get terribly involved with legal problems that resulted in jail time and personal injury? In a manner this angered Jay but the tears flowed anyway. His tears clouded his vision but he continued to drive. Jay recalled also that his father never drank alcohol. Jay was never very close to his father and angry feelings surfaced whenever he thought of him. Why? They never were really close and Jay recalled never being told he was loved by his father. All of this began to flood back to him. Why? His upbringing was what you might call strictly puritan. Children were to be seen, occasionally, and not heard. Things of a sexual nature were never brought to the light of day much less openly discussed. Jay began to recognize a pattern that developed with his father.

Jay drove and lost track of time. He arrived home and Kayce was waiting for him. He was eager to tell her what had happened in New Orleans and to share the details of the psychiatric evaluation. Before he could speak, Kayce said, "I've contacted WesterBrook and I have scheduled an appointment for you." Kayce watched for Jay's reactions but none were forthcoming. He simply requested for a cup of coffee and said to Kayce, "Sit down." Kayce sat down and wondered why Jay seemed so calm and controlled in this situation? Jay began, "I was thinking of doing that myself and I'm glad you called. When is it scheduled?" Kayce was awe struck at Jay's calm demeanor and his positive reaction to her statement. "Well, Friday morning at 9:00 A.M." At this point he shared with Kayce why he had really gone to New Orleans and went into specific details concerning the recommendations of Dr. Devere. Kayce began to get a clearer picture of the calm and positive demeanor. She did not share her feelings with Jay however. What worked to get him to WesterBrook was okay with her at this point. She was not forgiving; only glad that he had so readily agreed to keep the appointment she had made for him.

Jay arrived for his scheduled appointment and met with Thomas Writon, a Licensed Professional Counselor and a trained Assessment Diagnostician. After brief introductory remarks were exchanged, Thomas explained the process to Jay and the assessment began.

After approximately two hours the formal assessment process was completed. Thomas told Jay to take a break, meaning go to lunch and return to the office by 1:00 P.M. for a review and formal recommendations, if any. Jay agreed to the lunch break and agreed to return at the appointed hour. Jay returned to the office after lunch and was escorted directly to Thomas' office. "Mr. Writon will be with you shortly," the aide softly said to Jay. Less than five minutes passed when Thomas walked into the office. No small talk this time. He got right to the point and began to refer directly to the computer sheet in his right hand. Thomas then said, "After carefully reviewing all the information gathered during the two-hour assessment and based upon my knowledge of the disease of addiction, I strongly urge you to seek professional help with your alcohol dependency!" Jay was stunned by that remark but was able to maintain his composure. "What are your thoughts at this point," Thomas queried. Jay was unable to answer and Thomas continued without missing a beat. Thomas gave Jay a copy of the assessment summary sheet and Thomas requested that he read it thoroughly. Jay thought to himself, "Hell yes, I'll read it!" Thomas then allowed Jay ample time to review the summary saying that he would return shortly and answer any questions that he might have. Jay again agreed and Thomas quietly left the consultation room.

Jay read the summary word for word: "This is a 38 year old, married Caucasian male who is being assessed for alcohol dependency. He presently holds the position of City Attorney in LaPorte, Louisiana. This assessment revealed a 21-year history of alcohol use beginning at age 17 while in high school (experimental at first), progressing to weekend parties with copious amounts of alcohol being consumed while in college. He further reports decreased use of alcohol during Law School, however. After graduation and passing the state bar examination, Jay entered the United States Army where he was attached to the Adjutant General Corp. It was during this particular time that his use of alcohol escalated and progressively worsened. This marked the beginning of a pattern of daily use of alcohol. He categorically denies the use of any other type of mood or mind-altering drug. No difficulties are reported while he served in the military and was honorably discharged after five years with the rank of Major. He further states that upon being separated from the service, he relaxed and did little for almost three months. He reports the same pattern of alcohol use as indicated above, daily use, but not always to intoxication. During this time he began to formulate plans to open a private law practice which he did in August of 1973. Things were slow at first but business picked up and he built the practice into a highly successful venture until he was appointed to his present position. His drinking continued unabated throughout these years with little problems noted except for the continued comments of friends and family. They would comment on his total preoccupation with alcohol and of being drunk at inappropriate times and on social occasions embarrassing everyone and then he would deny the situation occurred. In the past six months he had received two DUI convictions and that wasn't motivation enough for him to stop using alcohol. Jay's social, occupational, and familial functioning was certainly indicative of the downward drift of the alcoholic in the late to middle stage of alcoholism. "No one ever approached me about my drinking" until I was convicted for those DUI citations and then no one really seemed to take it seriously," he dryly commented. Jay's use of alcohol has moved dramatically from "social drinking" through "abusive drinking" (drinking despite behavioral-social consequences) and finally to alcohol dependence (addiction).

The use of alcohol by Jay had become a socially safe outlet to allow him to be fully alive, to experience without being forced to hold himself accountable to anyone. For Jay, he continued, inappropriate use of alcohol has led to extreme loss of control and in the final analysis: This use has become "life-seeking" which allows him to be fully alive without the life of censure or castigation. Another aspect of Jay's disease of dependency to alcohol involves the concept of "risk-taking." His extreme sense of perfectionism thwarts his appropriate "risk-taking" attitudes and behaviors, thereby robbing him of the opportunity to be wondrously alive and truly spontaneous in his interactions with others. In a word, Jay, as a result of long-term alcohol use, has extreme difficulties with establishing and maintaining lasting personal relationships and he continues to seek these fulfilling relationships through the direct use of alcohol. Therefore, it is my professional opinion that this 38-year old male meets and fulfills diagnostic criteria for alcoholism as outlined in the Diagnostic Statistical Manual (DSM III-R) and I strongly recommend inpatient placement as soon as possible to focus on Jay's long standing difficulties. It is possible that Jay has been using alcohol in an attempt to self-medicate some of his pain or to correct these exhibited dysfunctions, yet he is addicted."

Chapter 6 - Kayce

After reading the summary, Jay was disgusted and angry but he could not disagree with what he had read. The lines on the summary bore heavily upon him. He had never seen his life laid out so succinctly. Jay felt the pangs of submission and surrender to the process but with a show of "forced resignation" rather than acceptance. His anger began to surface as Thomas reiterated the seriousness of the situation and again reminded him of the crisis that brought him to the assessment. Again Jay could not disagree. Thomas further remarked to him that he had been extremely lucky thus far and sooner or later, that "luck" would run out for him. Again he strongly urged Jay to be admitted without delay. Jay continued to be reticent and refused to make a commitment without talking with Kayce first. Jay agreed to call Thomas in the morning with a decision, and said goodbye, as he walked out of the office silently mumbling to himself.

Thomas returned to his chair. He thoughtfully replayed the assessment in his mind as he had on countless times in the past. This had been a "piece of cake" not at all like his assessment of the twenty-six year old black woman who was referred to him by the LaPorte Mental Health Department some months back. He occasionally referred to this as the "Twinkie assessment". His collateral information from the referral source stated "abuse of benzodiazepines" and they wanted her to be treated for dependency to the drug. She was accompanied by her Mother who displayed a somewhat strained facial expression. She related to me that the therapist at the Mental Health Center wanted her daughter to be treated for drug addiction but the Mother was certain other problems were present. I continued with my assessment until the receptionist called me to come to the front desk for just a minute. She had some information to relay to me that might be helpful in my evaluation. I excused myself and left the office leaving the Mother and daughter seated. Peggy simply told me that as the young woman was waiting to see me, she sat and methodically began to pluck the leaves from one of the office plants and was mumbling to herself. I expressed an appreciation for the information and returned to my office where I had left the young woman and her Mother. I took my chair and noticed that candy wrappers covered the carpet. Also I realized that she had taken my lunch bag (which included a Twinkie") and my hand-held tape recorder off my desk and was attempting to open the bag. Her Mother nonchalantly offered that her daughter had difficulty with "boundary setting" and "what belonged to her" and "what belonged to others." I retrieved the bag and recorder while she carried on a very animated conversation with the wall which included both sides of the rather bizarre conversation. At this point I suspected an impending psychotic break and I immediately called and made a referral to Hedgewood Psychiatric Hospital for stabilization and referral back to WesterBrook for the required drug treatment, if that was indeed required. Her Mother agreed to take her there immediately and both walked out of my office. I never heard from either of them again. I have often wondered what happened to that troubled young woman.

Jay got into his car and headed home along the all too familiar highway. But he then decided to stop by Budde's to see Shelby. He arrived at Budde's at 2:00 P.M. and after several drinks he again headed home. He hardly said two words to Shelby; another excuse to have a "couple for the road."

Arriving home late, he was greeted at the front door by Kayce. "Where have you been?" "Mr. Writon has called several times for you." "How did the assessment go?" "Have you been drinking again today?" With these statements Kayce responded in a frustrated manner, "What's the use!"

She angrily went to the bedroom and slammed the door shut. Jay heard the click of the lock. He stood motionless and frozen in time. Jay slowly sat down in the big overstuffed chair in his den. "Why do I continue to do this?" Jay was indeed having difficulty and for him the time had arrived when he could begin to accept it. The woman he loved and treasured had become second in his life and he knew what was first. Thus in this intervention enacted in a real-time life event, Jay's dependency and alcohol became apparent to him as he began to recognize the impact of alcohol use on major role obligations at work and home and how he had been giving up important social, occupational, and recreational pursuits in favor of his self-defeating relationship with alcohol. Indeed, he had been totally pre-occupied with his alcohol use: His "drug of choice!" Jay timidly walked from his den and headed toward the locked bedroom. It had been two hours and not a sound had been heard from the other side of the door. Softly he knocked on the door, "Kayce, let's talk, please!" He stood there in his shame and remorse waiting patiently for a reply that didn't come. He returned to his den and began to weep. Shortly he heard footsteps and looked up to meet the hurt-filled eyes of his wife. Kayce entered the den and stood just inside the doorway. Jay looked up at her. It was obvious he had been crying. This was nothing new to Kayce because Jay had used this ploy before to gain her sympathy. Still, his tears tore at her heart. "Jay, I just cannot go on like this anymore. Everything is getting out of hand. What is it going to take before you see that your drinking is destroying you and destroying us? Not six hours ago you left an evaluation session that was prompted by your use of alcohol and your resulting behaviors. What did you do? You stop by Budde's and come home stinking drunk. Dammit Jay, you've got to do something!"

Jay's anger that had been building for the past three weeks exploded, disinhibited by the alcohol consumed. The City EAP, the judge, Mr. Writon, Dr. Devere, and now Kayce were demanding that "he do something about the present situation." Through the drunken mist of his mind he saw himself stride across the floor and strike Kayce in the face with the back of his hand. She stumbled back and he grabbed her by the arms and shook her fiercely then shoved her away from him. Kayce fell backwards over the desk chair feeling the wood scrape her back, buttocks and legs. She scrambled up vaguely aware that Jay was approaching her. Her fear was such that she could hardly breathe. She had to get away! She bolted by Jay grabbing the car keys off the sofa table as she passed. She ran out of the house and realized only after she was in the car that she had neither her purse nor shoes on her feet. Sobbing as she drove, where was she going to go?

From the door, Jay watched the red tail lights of the BMW as she sped out of the driveway and down the street. He was still too drunk to realize the full implications of his actions but was aware that something dreadful had happened and that it was his fault. He loved Kayce so much, but why did his behavior indicate otherwise? Earlier today at Budde's, Shelby had been polite and friendly but reserved and somewhat distant. There had been little conversation. Jay was confused and exhausted. He went back to the den and sat down in his recliner. As sleep overtook him, Jay thought: I am tired of living like this. Maybe Writon is right. Hell, I'm willing to give it a try. I'll give anything a try at this point.

It was eight o'clock when the sounds of the doorbell awaken Jay. At first he was disorientated but then, with vivid recall, last night's events crashed in on him. The doorbell rang again and it seemed to be inside his head. He opened the front door to find Jon standing there. He could tell Jon was angry though Jon said nothing. "Come in Jon." Jon walked through the door and straight to the kitchen. Jay followed him and watched as Jon started the coffee maker. Jon said nothing until the coffee had brewed and he and Jay were sitting at the breakfast table with their coffee steaming in the cups. Just a few days ago he was sitting here with Kayce telling her about Jay's being in jail. Now, he sat facing Jay. "Jay, you and I have been friends for a long time. We have grown up together and faced all the trials and tribulations of that growth. Hell man, you are more of a brother to me than a best friend. What I have to say to you isn't going to be easy for either one of us. Kayce came by my place last night after her encounter with you. She was extremely upset and I let her stay until she felt she could drive safely. When she left, she went to your parents' house. I suppose she is still there. I gotta tell you, when I saw her bruised cheek, my first thought was to come over here and beat the living hell out of you. No woman deserves to be treated that way! I want you to know my advice to her. I told her to leave you until you got help for your drinking. I love you like a brother, but that lady is in danger until you get control of yourself! Jay had listened intently to Jon. His shoulders were sagging and his eyes were anguished. "Jon, I love Kayce more than anyone or anything. I can't lose her now. I'm willing to do anything, Jon do you hear me? I will do anything to keep her from leaving me." Jon stood up and started to the door, he turned around and walked back to Jay and put his arm around Jay's shoulders. Gently he said, "Call her at your Mother's and tell her that, Jay." Jay got up from the chair and walked to the door with Jon. At the door, Jon told Jay: "I've accepted the job in Alaska and will be leaving the end of the week. I'll touch base before I leave." Jay watched Jon leave and turned around and walked back to the den.

He sat at the desk staring at the phone. After a few minutes he picked up the receiver and dialed his Mother's number. Greta answered the phone on the third ring. "Greta, this is Jay, is my wife there?" "Just a minute, Mr. Jay, I'll get your wife." Shortly, Jay heard Kayce's soft "Hello." "Kayce, I know you've heard this a thousand times before, but I'm sorry about last night. You are right; I must do something to control my drinking. I just want you to know that as soon as

I hang up from talking with you, I'm calling WesterBrook for admission. Kayce, I love you, I need you. Please go with me to WesterBrook." Kayce listened to Jay. She felt tired to her very bones. She didn't want to go with Jay; she didn't want to make any commitments but remembered her promise to Jon last night. "Ok, Jay, but I'm staying with your parents. I'm not coming home just now. Bye Jay." As Jay cradled the receiver, he thought "Well the die is cast. I'll just have to wait and see where this all leads." He got up and made his way to the shower and then to bed alone. He would call Mr. Writon in the morning with his decision to be admitted to WesterBrook.

After talking with Thomas, Jay agreed to be admitted the morning of the next day. Mr. Writon wanted him there by 9:00 A.M. and Jay agreed. He called Kayce and told her the details. "Will you ride over there with me, please?" At last Kayce agreed and Jay would pick her up at 7:00 A.M. He told her thanks and good night.

Chapter 7 - The Treatment Facility

WesterBrook was located at the mouth of a box canyon in the wilds of Louisiana Cajun country, forty miles from the nearest city. "Isolated," he thought. A pristine forest surrounded the out buildings with a rippling brook, always bubbling along, and coursing through the middle of the property. When he stopped a few miles back at the country store, the man there stated, "that place up there covers 175 acres, looks like they could find something else to do with that much land; nothing but a bunch of alcoholics and drug addicts in there; they are a nuisance to the community." But, to continue, a lake was located just north of the Unit and fishing was allowed, he understood. He had brought his fly-rig with him, just in case that information was correct. The buildings were rustic and seemed to issue a warm invitation to sit and stay awhile. Mr. Writon had told him at least sixty patients could be accommodated at one time and that seemed like a lot of people to be in one place for the same condition.

He glanced over toward Kayce and she seemed to be a million miles away, lost in her thoughts. Kayce was fully aware that Jay wanted to engage in small talk but she refused the invitation. She was angry and frustrated but a gnawing feeling that she should be at least glad for this trip, kept merging with her anger. "Hold your tongue for now," she thought silently to herself. Hurt kept rising mixed with a sense of dread and uncertainty. He didn't interrupt Kayce's chosen silence and returned to his driving chores and keeping track of all the turns and twists in the narrow paved road. After rounding a curve, he saw the grand entrance of WesterBrook and the big sign that seemed to beckon him. WesterBrook was stately yet appeared warmly inviting as Jay and Kayce drove up the winding drive toward the front entrance. Bradford Pear trees lined the drive and they were blooming with life and fragrance. Jay silently thought to himself, as if prompted by the sight of the life of the blooming trees, that maybe he could grow here also! The winding road leading to WesterBrook was littered with broken relationships, unfulfilled promises, emotional hurts, and dreams that had become a gray mist in the darkness of addiction. For the past nine months he had felt an estrangement from the woman who had accompanied him on this journey. He felt a deep sense of sadness but he could not gather the emotional strength to articulate it. His intellect could not reconcile those past events or the behaviors that gushed forth from the depths of his drinking. These remained with Jay as he got out of the car and stood surveying the look of the place. Both he and Kayce silently questioned what was to come as they walked through the big double doors leading to the reception area. Sherry, a staff member, greeted them at the door. She would escort Jay to the assessment and admission office. Another staff member met with Kayce. Jay and Kayce then parted with each headed in a different direction. This seemed all too familiar to Jay. Ross, the Family Program Representative, explained some of the process to her including details of the family involvement that was expected at WesterBrook. She listened quietly as the staff member droned on and on about "the mysteries of the place." By this time, Kayce had a strong desire to quickly leave this place that had now engulfed her life and husband. She felt a twinge of anger welling up inside. She had had about enough! The past two months had been hell and now this, this person was telling her she was expected to stay a week at this place. The very idea of spending more than an hour here was unthinkable. Why had she ever mentioned this place? When the Judge ordered the psychiatric evaluation, she had no idea that the results would recommend WesterBrook. Well, here she was, and she didn't like it a bit. Ross, the Family Program Representative, was saying "Mrs. Bienville are you agreeable to Family Week?" Kayce looked at the man. He looked harmless enough but also looked very insincere. “Yes, yes, of course” (maybe she would come down with the flu or something). “Also, Mrs. Bienville, you will be required to attend the family group meetings each week and one Alanon meeting. After all, Mrs. Bienville, this is a family disease we are dealing with.” “Bull shit!” Kayce was surprised at herself; the only swearing she used was “dammit.” But all of this was a little much for her. By the time Jay had agreed to “treatment” Kayce had decided that she wanted a divorce. The only thing that had stopped her was her promise to Jon. Kayce let her thoughts wander back to the last time she saw Jon.

She had gone to Jon after Jay started drinking again. Jay’s last drinking bout had ended with his beating her. Kayce had left the house with nothing except what she was wearing. She did not even have on her shoes. After driving around for an hour or so she had gone to Jon. Crying, she told him everything and he was so kind. As he held her, she felt safer and more at peace than she had felt in years. With defeat and gratitude in her eyes she looked up at Jon. He drew a shaky breath and she knew he was going to kiss her. Kayce did not lower her face. She waited for his kiss. Jon looked down at Kayce. He saw the bruised cheek and felt her wince as he put his arms around her. Her green eyes looked like emeralds floating in crystal water. He loved this woman and knew he was going to kiss her. He felt her surrender and was lost. Gently he kissed her and lifted her to the bedroom. Slowly, he undressed her. Anger surged through him as he saw angry red welts on her arms, back and legs. He silently swore he would love gently, taking time to meet her needs but as she received him, he knew this time would be quick. He had dreamed of this so many nights. “I’m so sorry Kayce, next time will be just for you.” And it was. Kayce did not know making love could be like this. With Jay it was one sided and usually she was left frustrated. But Jon gently and patiently brought her to heights of passion she never knew she could reach. She fell asleep on his shoulder. As Jon watched her sleep, he knew he must take the Alaska offer. Too much damage and hurt had already taken place. He was standing by the window and turned to see Kayce watching him from the bed. Softly she said "Jon, I'm going to ask Jay for a divorce." Jon took a deep breath and firmly spoke the hardest words he had ever spoken in his life. "Let me do this right, Lord" he silently prayed. "Kayce, don't ask if I love you and don't tell me you love me. These things can't be spoken for if they are, we both are lost. I know Jay loves you and that you once loved him. He needs you now more than ever but you can't stay with him until he gets something done about his drinking. He is going to hurt you badly if you don't get out. I'll never forget this afternoon but I must ask you to. Kayce, if you must divorce Jay, do it after he is well. He loves you. Use it to make him get help. Promise me you won't divorce him before he gets help." Kayce promised. She wondered how Jon liked Alaska.

"Mrs. Bienville, Mrs. Bienville!" Yes, Ross, what were you saying? Ross patiently repeated to Kayce that their interview was over and that she could see Jay before she left, if she wanted to. Kayce declined the offer and left as Ross told her she would be hearing from them concerning the weekly meetings, Alanon, and family week.

Kayce started the drive from WesterBrook alone back to LaPorte. What was that Ross said? A family disease! Well, what did he know? The idea was so absurd. Kayce felt a great deal of hostility and resentment and, to be perfectly honest, very afraid. Why, that insipid man even insinuated that Kayce thought Jay's drinking was her fault! This next month was going to be a real trip: A trip that Kayce was not looking forward to in the least. He mentioned that in the family group as well as the Alanon meetings "everyone would share their experiences" in order to help the other group members. If they thought she was going to air her family's dirty laundry to a bunch of people she didn't know, they were absolutely insane. What in the world had she gotten herself into? Glancing down at the schedule on the seat she saw that the first Alanon was next Wednesday evening. Wednesday should be very interesting!

Chapter 8 - Kayce and Alanon

Kayce was nervous as she drove to her first Alanon meeting. She thought about the beginning of this gathering of people. It seems that family members of alcoholics needed the same type of group support that alcoholics got from Alcoholics Anonymous (AA), Kayce surmised. So, Alanon was born. And, all of this took place decades ago. Kayce supposed it was a well-kept secret because she never heard of it until Jay went to treatment. She turned onto the grounds of WesterBrook and glanced at her watch. Ah, she was on time. Kayce planned it just right because she didn't want to be too early nor did she want to enter after the meeting had begun. She wanted to be as "unnoticed" as possible. The group of about nine people was going into the room just as Kayce walked up. She noticed that the room was rather non-descriptive and there was no particular decor. Chairs were assembled in a semicircle and everyone was beginning to sit down. Kayce quietly observed the collection of people. There was a rather made up woman whose name was Marla, a powder blonde named Dottie, Carmen, who was mousey-looking, and Michelle who had already began to cry. The men were no less interesting. James was tall, good looking, and easy going. Kenith was plump and had a look of desperation about him. Dan was the quiet one who seemed to be smoldering, and then there was Jake. It was obvious that Jake was the kind who was always on the prowl. Kayce made a mental note to stay out of Jake's way. The most intriguing was Mr. Myrtle.

Kayce chuckled to herself as she assessed him. If she hadn't known better, she would have sworn he had just stepped out of the 1850's. She guessed him to be about sixty-five. He had white hair, a goatee, wore a light tan suit, and carried a cane and dress hat. His eyes were periwinkle blue and seemed to twinkle. She wondered what on earth he was doing at this type of meeting. If anyone in the world had a look of serenity, Mr. Myrtle wore it with ease and style. Marla was calling the meeting to order (while making a great to do about the group not being organized). She announced to the group that there were two new attendees, and to Kayce's dismay, named Kayce and James. Kayce nodded and James just smiled. After the introduction, Marla asked if anyone had anything special to share with the group and Michelle said, very tearfully, that she wasn't sure she was going to make it. She believed everything was her fault and that she was afraid of her husband but wasn't sure she really wanted him to stop drinking. At this point, both Marla and Dottie embarked on personal experiences of their own and in no time everyone was telling his or her own version of a similar happening. It seemed that each person's story got bigger and better (or perhaps lower and worse was a better phrase) than the one before. James and Kayce just looked at each other. Mr. Myrtle was watching the two of them. Mrs. Bienville looked horrified and Mr. Woodrow looked amazed. Having been a member of this particular Alanon group for five years, Mr. Myrtle always found newcomers amusing. He recalled when he realized that his beloved Lucinda would never stop drinking, that he had called WesterBrook. They had treated him with dignity and concern. They told him about Alanon and had invited him to the weekly meeting held there. They even helped him with an intervention with Miss Lucy. Unfortunately, it did not work for Lucinda adamantly refused to go to treatment there. A southern lady might have a nervous stomach, a nervous breakdown or some other "acceptable" malady; but to ask her to admit to something as crude as alcoholism was unthinkable. Alcoholics were those poor unfortunate wretches lying along the riverbank. Of course, Miss Lucy had never seen one (not that she would admit to anyway) a lady's sensibilities would be outraged to actually see such, but she had heard about them. No, she certainly was not in need of any "help" for her drinking, thank you. And do not mention it again! He never said another word to his Miss Lucy (he had called Lucinda "Miss Lucy" ever since their courting days) but thanks to this group of odd people, Myron Myrtle lived his life in laughter, love, peace and serenity. Mrs. Bienville was going to need his help. Mr. Myrtle made a silent commitment to be there for her when she was ready to let it all go.

Chapter 9 - Treatment at WesterBrook

The schedule of the treatment center was explained to him in detail upon the completion of the admission process. The last time that he had signed that many pieces of paper was when he and Kayce bought their $240,000 house with a mortgage of thirty years. But he was now a "patient" and they referred to him as a "patient". "Funny," he thought. The admission clerk further told him that his counselor was Bobby Gandaff and this counselor would be meeting with him later today. He was escorted to the Nursing Station where a great deal of activity was occurring. The Charge Nurse called for Physician's Orders to admit Jay to the Detoxification Unit. After contact was made, the order was written for the Medical Director's signature. Additionally, Dr. Price had previously instructed the nurse on duty to begin the regimen of Naltrexone on the next two admissions, specifically if both were "alcoholic." Jay and the newly admitted man in the other room would be the two subjects involved. One would be given the Naltrexone medication and the other given a placebo. Both men were alcoholic, about the same age and physical condition, and were admitted with an extended history of alcohol use. This drug was known to block the pleasurable effects of those opiate-like substances in the brain that were released by alcohol that showed a potential to help the problem drinker stay sober. Also separate studies indicated the drug was an effective agent in long-term sobriety through this blocking action. Both men were advised of the medication to be used in their detoxification regimen. Neither objected to the detoxification medications. Both knew other medications would be used in conjunction with their detoxification. The Naltrexone regimen would begin after the initial injection of Phenobarbitol and thiamine. The Medical Director would monitor these specific two admissions via the questionnaires that would be mailed out to them at intervals of 3 months, 6 months, 9 months, 18 months, and 24 months. These questionnaires were the same as those mailed to all patients therefore nothing special needed to be explained to them. Dr. Price was hoping to duplicate the other twin studies to validate the usefulness of Naltrexone with alcoholic patients.

Jay was instructed to take a seat and that a nurse would be right with him to take his "vital signs." He calmly sat down and waited. His vital signs were within normal limits except for a slightly elevated blood pressure reading and his blood alcohol level was .00. He had consumed no alcohol for the past two days and he subjectively reported that he felt physically fine. His objective vital signs validated that report. Additionally, urine and blood chemistry profiles would be completed with a scheduled appointment set with the Medical Director to complete a History and Physical examination. The History and Physical examination is the instrument utilized in clinically justifying appropriateness for treatment and level of care. The History and Physical examination will further state pertinent findings of relevant clinical importance that clearly communicates across all disciplines. The physician will also record and highlight any emerging clinical problems that, in the physician's judgment, require further clinical evaluation and/or treatment. The Medical Director will also review the lab work and document any abnormalities found. Jay was told by the nurse on duty that when the blood and urine chemistry profiles returned from the laboratory, the Medical Director would review them with him. That was agreeable, Jay thought. After the blood was drawn by the nurse on duty, he was requested to take a cup to the restroom and bring it back as soon as possible. Jay followed orders explicitly and proudly presented the cup to the nurse. Next, he was instructed to return to his assigned detox bed and rest. This Jay was glad to do.

Another staff member knocked and entered his room and explained to Jay that he wanted to present the admission kit to him which included "the Big Book," the 12 and 12, the 24-hours a day meditation book, paper, pen, and a copy of all the papers he had signed in the admission office. And what was that "big book" the aide referred to earlier, a bunch of Bible thumpers probably. Jay thought, well, why not! Jay then asked, "Sherry, what is your understanding of this disease of alcoholism I keep hearing so much about?" She looked deeply into Jay's eyes and said, "sit down for a minute and I'll tell you some of my ideas." Jay sat down promptly and awaited her reply. She walked over to the window and slowly began.

"Your use of alcohol can be attributed to one of the following or possibly a combination of all three: Number one, to overcome unwanted feelings or emotions, number two, to provide a new, exciting, or stimulating experience, or number three, to satisfy peer influence. This use will continue until it's discontinued by personal choice or the individual crosses the wall to addiction. And once there, he can no longer return to social, asymptomatic use of alcohol. He is alcoholic. I am aware that in the beginning you viewed alcohol use as a purely acceptable social behavior and you did not view it as some type of deviant behavior. You did not wake up one bright, sunny morning, peer out your bedroom window and make a decision then and there to become the very best alcoholic you could possibly be. It doesn't work that way. It becomes so as the wall to alcoholism and addiction is crossed. The alcoholic generally associates only with those who use alcohol in the same way he does and thus this interaction validates and re-enforces each other's use and behaviors. Little time is devoted to interpersonal relationships outside this vicious circle.

As the disease progresses, drinking alone seems to dominate your use. You have no close friends! In way you have drank them all away! Jay could personally identify and validate these hard statements. He was learning more and more and like a hungry, dry sponge, the information was being soaked into his very soul. Jay was beginning to discover, ever so slowly, that he had been lost in his use of alcohol for a long time, maybe even back to his pre-adolescent years. Somehow through his experimentations he found the aesthetic properties of alcohol use and he had found the magical elixir of social intercourse. Anxieties lifted, his life was more energized. Others did not matter as much; Only Jay and his unrealistic expectations of life, always with alcohol as a constant companion and healer. Was the time now, he thought. Sherry moving the book on her desk regained his attention. Sherry said further, "All the information about yourself and about the disease of dependency won't keep you sober! Much work and action on your part will be required, much more like a deeply internalized commitment to a new way of living and relating. The question is not so much why the alcoholic drinks the way he does; it is why he has such an inordinate desire to flee from self, to take on another persona, a new personality. What's dysfunctional with the present self? It becomes a fear of being themselves and/or the clutching at another role in life. Where does that originate? For that existential question, I have no answer, Jay. However, I do know that frequently the alcoholic wants, and at various times demands, answers to his dysfunctional life that will allow him to feel better while continuing to maintain the same patterns and relationships that are exacerbating the dysfunction in the first place."

Jay would ponder that statement for a while. Jay thanked Sherry for her time and the information she had given him. Jay was very impressed with the amount of knowledge for one who was so young, who seemed to intuitively "know" what he was feeling, and who had the ability to actively interact verbally with him.

Soon the duty nurse came into his room and gave him an injection of thiamine and two hundred forty milligrams (240 mg IM) of Phenobarbitol. (While in the detoxification phase, he would receive titrated doses of Phenobarbitol to ward off any impending withdrawal symptoms. Throughout the treatment process he would be administered a mega-vitamin and the Naltrexone.) The needle stick hurt like hell but he did not allow the nurse to know that she had hurt him. The nurse turned to Jay and said, "get some rest because tomorrow will be a busy day for you."

The nurse had not observed hard signs of the alcoholic withdrawal syndrome such as profuse sweating, anxiety coupled with irritability and agitation, abnormal vital signs, and hyperactivity. She knew Jay was in fairly good physical health when compared to his admitted history of alcohol use and that DT's were unlikely. But she knew the syndrome could appear up to seventy-two hours after the last use of alcohol. And she was being cautious. Jay was being assessed according to his physiological indicators (B/P, pulse, respirations, temperature, etc.) as a requirement for medication and not solely according to his subjective reports or requests. The time was 9:00 P.M. and the Medical Director entered his room accompanied by the nurse on duty.

It was time to complete the History and Physical Examination and Jay obliged. After forty-five minutes the ordeal was over. The Medical Director, Ron Price, then took the opportunity to review the lab results with Jay. Several enzymes were elevated including Glucose 131 (70-110 normal), SGOT (AST) 41 (0-37), Uric Acid 11.1 (3.4-7.0), Total Protein 8.7 (5.4-7.4), Creatinine 1.5 (.6-1.3), and MCV 98.4 (80-94). Jay wanted to know, at this point, what those various numbers represented and was there any cause for alarm? Dr. Price assured Jay that these elevations were indicative of the alcoholic patient and they should return to baseline levels very soon. The SGOT elevation indicated some inflammation of the liver but nothing to be that concerned about, if he quit drinking alcohol! The MCV and SGOT elevations are considered by many research scientists in the field of addictive diseases to be positive genetic and medical markers for the disease of alcoholism. "The statistics are quite impressive," the Doctor remarked. Jay felt somewhat relieved and returned to his bed.

As he was dropping off to sleep, a strange feeling enveloped him: a calmness that he had lost years before was allowing someone to instruct "him" for the first time in many years. It felt good. Sleep overtook him and he slept peacefully and free of those "chaotic" dreams. The nurse came into the room several times during the night to check on Jay and each time he was sleeping soundly and appeared to be having a restful night. He was not sweating or tossing or turning in the bed. This was the routine throughout his first night in the treatment center. He awoke and felt refreshed but sadness overtook him and he lay there in the bed and cried for the first time in a long time.

The nurse entered the dimly lit room with another injection of Phenobarbital for Jay and his first dose of Naltrexone. He cringed when he saw the needle and turned over on his side. After the injection, the aide on duty brought his breakfast to him and he gladly took the tray and nibbled at the food prepared for him. After breakfast, he watched two detox-oriented videos. After each one, the aide on duty would enter the lounge area and help him to process the primary subject of the video and what it meant specifically to him. He continued to feel physically OK but these events were beginning to extract a toll on him psychologically. Toward the late evening, he began to feel somewhat nauseated and his head began to ache. He rang for the nurse to bring him some medication for the nausea and Motrin for his headache. After approximately ten minutes, she arrived with the medication for him and another scheduled injection of Phenobarbital, which was to be his last.

Sleep overcame him easily but there were interruptions. His newly arrived roommate was having a difficult time with his detoxification. Jay was somewhat awake when the staff brought him into the room and Jay could hear him mumbling. Nothing he said could be understood. He appeared to be well over sixty years old and from what he could gather as a result of an overheard conversation, the man had a long history of alcohol use and several previous treatment attempts. Jay also heard one of the nursing staff mention that Anthony might also be experiencing pre-senile dementia that was being exacerbated by his continuous use of alcohol. He heard them mention that Anthony was not able to repeat the "Babcock Sentence," whatever that was. Later the nurse told him: "The one thing a nation needs in order to be rich and great is a large secure supply of wood." Jay thought that rather strange. The nurse did not explain that this intervention was a way of measuring short-term memory deficits that are characteristic of the patient with dementia. Additionally, the smell was terrible as the patient was escorted into the room. The nursing staff had some concerns that Anthony (the new patient) might develop severe withdrawal symptomatology that could result in delirium tremens (DTs) with the potential of a stroke, seizures, and death. Up to this point, Jay had taken his detoxification program lightly, but now he began to be concerned for this older man in the bed next to his. Jay was glad to know that the "older" population could now be properly diagnosed with alcoholism and not just some type of pre-senile or senile dementia or some other psychiatric disorder. Anthony seemed so dejected and lethargic and he rarely spoke and seemed to be in a bad mood for much of the time he had been his roommate.

The third day dawned for Jay and it appeared that his new roommate was going to be all right with his detoxification. Anthony tossed and turned all night and this continued to interrupt Jay's sleep. Jay felt like he had been awake all night but the thoughts of getting out of this extreme medical environment pleased him; so he did not complain about his restless night. This day meant that he would be transferred to the Rehab phase of treatment and he was glad to hear that news. That meant "no more shots!"

After breakfast, another staff member knocked and entered his room. This staff member would help Jay move to the assigned Rehab cottage. Jay gathered up all his "stuff." He said bye to Anthony wishing him a speedy detox and then proceeded to follow the young woman to Cottage "Delta." He walked into the cottage and was greeted by the other residents. They welcomed him and attempted to make him feel at home. Jay half-heartedly shared in their extended feinted enthusiasm. No one felt that good; especially not in a treatment center for alcoholics and drug-addicts." The cottage group leader extended his hand and Jay graciously shook the hand offered him. He was then assigned to a room and told where he could store his personal items. The cottage leader then reviewed the cottage rules and Jay agreed to abide by them. The aide then explained to Jay that an inspection and inventory of his personal items was the next chore on the list. Jay began to unpack his suitcase and the aide on duty watched very carefully as each item was unpacked. He also closely examined the clothes as Jay hung them neatly in the closet. It was 8:30 A.M. by the time he was settled into his assigned room that was to be his "home" for the next few days.

The aide explained to Jay that he was to be in group room "A" at 9:15 A.M. for his first group session. There, he would also meet his Primary Counselor, Bobby Gandaff. (Bobby Gandaff has been with WesterBrook for eight of his thirteen years experience in the alcohol and drug treatment industry. He is a Certified Addictions Counselor, married, and the father of two young boys, ages seven and eight. His primary motivation for entering this particular profession was attributable to his alcoholic father. He participated in all the Family Activities during his father's treatment and he knew he had found his vocation. Presently he is working on his undergraduate degree and has plans for graduate school after graduation. He began his new vocation in the Crisis Response Unit of a State Supported Facility in LaPorte, Louisiana and steadily moved up to his present position of "Primary Counselor." Bobby, while he doesn't have his degree yet, has worked very hard in getting his certification in the field of addiction including attendance of seminars and many hours of "burning the midnight oil" in self-education. He has read extensively especially the theory and therapy of Carl Rogers and his Client-Centered approach to change and therefore growth. He adopted three conditions out of his readings for human growth, which were evident in his therapeutic interactions: 1. Genuineness or congruence (to experience what the patient is experiencing), 2. Positive regard (unconditional acceptance without judgment), and 3. Empathetic understanding (feelings of being understood by another person). During the intervening years however he adopted the educational, directive, active stance espoused by Albert Ellis in his Rational Emotive Therapy. Bobby integrated it within the Rogerian framework and this style seemed to bring better results, especially with the addictive population. Bobby also made use of metaphors and some hypnotic techniques of Milton Erickson. Additionally, he liked Erickson's description and the use of values through the evaluation of the patient's thinking style, response style and attention style. Further, he was keenly aware of the power that was attributed to him being a Primary Counselor and Group Leader. Concomitantly, the group, and to a lesser extent, the individual patient, somehow felt weak and ineffectual, impotent, ignorant, and powerless. In addition, a magical belief was ordinarily bestowed upon the Counselor that he could understand perfectly and could resolve all issues that might arise. Therefore, with the above ideas in mind, within his formal and self-education efforts, "Primum Non Nocere," the injunction to "first, do no harm" became a guiding beacon for him in his interactions with those patients entrusted to his care. Bobby could feel the pain of addiction as readily as any addict as the result of his co-dependency issues associated with his father's addiction.

He was a caring, kind, gentle, and considerate man as attested to by the following letter he received recently from one of his previous patients and it reads as follows:

"Dear Bobby:

You may be surprised to be hearing from me, a former patient and "pesky alcoholic!" Remember me? I want to inform you that I have stayed with the Program of AA, working the Steps, reading the Traditions, reading the "Big Book" and attending AA meetings on a daily basis. I received my six-month "chip" last Wednesday night. My son, friends, and family are so happy for me. I also have been working on my character defects and shortcomings, trying to act in an adult, unselfish way and being a "Lady" like I used to be. Thank-you for all you did for me and also thank the Nursing staff and Doctor Price for me. Also tell Sherry I said hello for me. I know that working with alcoholics and drug addicts must be tiring at times. May God bless you all! You saved my life. Tell Dr. Price thanks for me. Bobby, I have kept all the appointments you arranged and I am going to live in spite of everything. I have looked to God, my Higher Power as I understand Him, and I turned my life and will over to Him. I attend Sunday school and Church on a regular basis. I stay quite busy. I walk 3 to 5 miles a day and I've gained five pounds and I feel wonderful. I feel I have so much to live for. I felt my life was over when I got to WesterBrook. Pray for me and keep your fingers crossed for six more months and I can have a sober one-year birthday in the AA Program. I'll be sixty-six years old on July 4, 1991 and I feel like a kid again! Good luck to you, your work, and your future! From a grateful recovering alcoholic.

Evelyn B."

Thus, this was Bobby Gandaff: A dedicated professional who always made it a practice to know his assigned patients and in the "knowing," the relationship was allowed to flourish thus initiating a solid foundation for growth and change to emerge.

Chapter 10 – The Milieu of Treatment

Jay promptly walked into the sparsely decorated group room as requested, accompanied by the rest of assigned group members. Two other people followed and after they had taken seats, the man introduced himself as Bobby Gandaff, the Primary Counselor assigned to the group. The other person who accompanied Bobby introduced herself as Janice Babiak, the co-Facilitator of the group. Bobby then said as a matter of passing, "The purpose of this group is not so much to give you answers and provide information, but more to help you explore and better understand feelings and situations that you find difficult to manage, and to better understand where you fit in with the difficulties that you experience." Further comments were made regarding individual confidentiality within the context of the group: "What is said in group, stays in group, and is not to be carried outside the group." The counselor seemed sincere enough, but Jay remained reserved and very much detached. Others had been there longer and it seemed they found it quite easy to talk about themselves.

This first group session was anxiety provoking for him and he doubted whether he would ever get anything out of this group. Jay did not handle anxiety very well and coupled with his lack of patience and his intolerance, he, at times, would simply rebel. He began to retreat to the safety of the past when his anxiety level dictated it and this was certainly one of those situations. He felt uneasy in this group and he felt they could see right to the very core of his being. His paranoia was working overtime again. He felt as if each one was slowing dissecting him. Thoughts of social engineering entered uninvited. This was, to his way of thinking, using group pressures in various disguises to change individual behaviors and attitudes. Was that being done and is that how those so-called “steps” worked? He wondered! This guy appeared competent but he was not a psychiatrist and Jay did not trust his intimate “self” with a “lay-person.” He found later that Bobby was a “Certified Addictions Counselor” and maybe that would be acceptable to him. Anyway he would wait and see. The group session was scheduled daily for ninety minutes and each second of this initial group session seemed agonizingly slowed.

After the counselor’s initial presentation (And it appeared that this was part of opening the group daily) he covered the “group rules’ which included a commitment to attend each session, to participate rather than comply, to offer feedback to others, that physical violence would neither be tolerated nor would threats of violence, to speak in the terms of the “here and now,” and further agree to remain seated throughout the group session. Jay had heard the counselor also use the term “confrontation” and within this context he was unsure of its meaning. He questioned the counselor about this “confrontation.” Bobby replied in an unconcerned manner: “Confrontation is simply holding a mirror up in front of your “self.” That mirror might be another peer remarking about your behavior or I might be the one “holding the mirror.” “You may not like what you “see” or in the process hear!” Bobby recognized manipulation when he heard it and braced for the attack that didn’t happen. Bobby knew that the goal of confrontation was not to get the patient “to admit to addiction or anything else” but rather to help him or her and the group to look squarely at what is going on in the “here and now,” with the specific aim of providing a better understanding of the behavior observed, promoting growth, and when necessary, in making changes. The counselor in this case identified his task as primarily to invite and encourage discussion among the various group members thus providing the environment for change and growth: Growth not only for the group but growth for the individual as well. Additionally Bobby explained to the assembled group that "group focuses on common concerns and personal issues and the very fact of his being a member of the group and seeking help was a positive step for Jay."

Jay then internalized that being a part of a group of people with similar problems and all seeking and needing help might lessen his severe anxiety. With all of that being presented by the counselor, Jay figured he could stay within the established boundaries. After all, he had finished high school, completed four years of college and law school, and served five years in the Army Security Agency attached to the Adjutant General Section, this should be a picnic. During this initial session, Jay continued to listen intently to every word Bobby uttered. He had been trained to listen with his mind and with his ear and this had been an invaluable aid to him in the past and now it might prove to be useful once again. A weak spot was worth ferreting out. He must have an edge, the "upper hand" and Jay would find a way to get to this "lay-person" even though he was a "Certified Addictions Counselor." Hell, I'm the professional here, Jay said to himself, almost arrogantly. As he sat there, another group norm developed, he thought, and it involved stating your name and problem as a prelude to the formalized group discussion. Jay patiently waited his turn and replied, "My name is Jay and I'm an alcoholic." That seemed to meet with everyone's approval and he was becoming less anxious now. Bobby glanced over toward Jay. "Welcome to the group Jay. We are glad you are here. Can you tell us a little about yourself?" Jay responded with a brief explanation of his presence but he was very cautious and gave them very sparse information.

Jay counted nine members in the group including himself. Six were males, and three were females. One of the females was a "real cutie" and behaved quite innocently and appeared to be extremely naive. His mind was not on the discussed "group process" but on how he could manipulate these other eight "members." Again his legal training took control and the thought of the many times he had been successful in manipulating a jury of twelve. This, indeed, would be a piece of cake, he mused lightheartedly. But normal self-consciousness, inhibitions about exposure and ordinary embarrassment are some factors which interfere with participating actively in the group process and Jay was no exception even though he normally enjoyed being before a group a people and being in the limelight. This was different because now he was the "limelight" and that did not feel good. He felt as if his very soul was on display in that group room and others at any minute could attack his already decreased self-esteem and self-confidence. His cleverly concealed facade was at risk and that scared him! His anxiety was growing.

Jay began to assign short "titles" or "nicknames" to each of the group members and in this way he would react to the description and stay clear of any type of emotional entanglements and traps. The following identifies the group members as Jay saw them: Shane – "the know it all," Jennifer – "the secretive one," Rene – "the cutie," Jackson – "the philosopher," Howard – "the lost child," Janet – "the rescuer," Gayland – "the clown," and David – "the scapegoat"/"the troubled one."

When the group session ended, Bobby walked over toward Jay. Jay wondered, "What's next?" Bobby advised him that after lunch he would schedule an individual session for information gathering and treatment planning. With that, Bobby disappeared in the mass of people that now filled the hallway. What time? Where? These seemingly important questions remained unanswered for the time being.

The next activity on the schedule was lunch, cafeteria style. Hospital food had a certain reputation that preceded his visit to this fine establishment and he did not look forward to this meal. But to his surprise, the food was presented in a very attractive manner. Adequate servings were available and it tasted just fine, "tasty." So far, so good! Again the food tasted good and lots of social interaction was observed at the various tables. Primary subjects of discussion included complaining about how staff members were insincere and didn't really care, how they were manipulating the counselors or nursing staff, some were bragging about "faking their seeming acceptance through being "yes persons," and the old "stay-by" sexual exploits, fantasies, and conquests. Jay nodded toward Rene and she quickly turned away. With that Jay picked up his tray to deposit the remains. That chore being completed, he headed for the patio and a much needed cigarette.

He sat down on one of the concrete benches and lit a cigarette. Looking up he saw Rene coming toward him. Surprised would be the word for the moment. She casually walked over to him and asked for a cigarette. After lighting it for her, she too sat down on the bench beside him. "Jay, I've been here fourteen days. The others are dull-brained and slime-balls, who are here because the court ordered them because they got into legal difficulties, or their families brought them here, or their employer forced them to be here. None of them has any degree of motivation to improve their alcoholic or drug-addicted lives. All they talk is bullshit! I want my life to improve and I'm sick and tired of being sick and tired. And I believe you want that for yourself. Is that right?" Jay sat on the concrete bench with his head down dumbfounded and unable to utter a word. He just nodded affirmatively, got up slowly, and walked toward his assigned cottage.

For an instant Jay became lost in the past and this approach by Rene reminded him of Shelby and the illicit relationship for the past ten years. Jay recognized that certain behaviors became socially acceptable, at least partially, when it was carried out under the influence of alcohol. The Steps, he was being taught, recommended strongly that amends be made to those he had hurt and Kayce was one of those he had certainly hurt. He indeed loved her and wanted his life with her. This way of living and relating must come to a stop! Jay would always remember how his use of alcohol had become the central organizing principle around which his whole life had been built. The use of alcohol and its effects had become more important in his life than people and this thought deeply saddened him. That would change!

Jay was learning more and more of this disease that existed for the sole purpose of killing him and any relationship that meant anything to him. As a result of the many detoxification videos that he had viewed and reviewed, with the aide on duty, he knew at an intellectual level now and beyond any doubt, that alcohol is a powerful "drug" whose psychopharmacological properties made it possible for both transient (short lived) stimulant and subsequent depressant effects that included major memory disturbances, mood lability, impaired cognitive abilities, created severe sleep disturbances, and socio-familial verbal barrages that could result in physical violence.

"Well, I guess I'll see you later," Rene yelled after him. This comment brought him instantly back to the present. "Yeah, see you later" Jay called back. Rene thought this action rather strange as she sat there and finished her cigarette. And this all the more intrigued her about Jay. "He didn't even try to hit on me," she remarked to herself softly.

Jay had just arrived back to his assigned cottage and sat down in one of the chairs on the porch when his counselor walked up the front steps. "How was lunch, Jay?" Jay remarked that it was better than he had expected it to be or not as bad as he imagined it might have been. "Great!" Bobby replied. Bobby also went on to explain that various assessments would be completed during the first week in treatment beginning with the medical aspects, covered in the History and Physical Examination and the Nursing Assessment, and followed by the Dietary Assessment by the Registered Dietitian, the Leisure-time Activities Assessment by the Activities Coordinator, and the Spiritual Assessment by the Chaplain. Then Bobby said, "Jay I have scheduled an hour or so with you this afternoon at 4:00 P.M. to complete the psychosocial assessment." Jay inquired, "What is this psychosocial "assessment" business and why is it necessary'? Bobby then continued. "Basic information is gathered and various assessments are formulated to identify problematic situations which have caused dysfunction or personal dissatisfaction within your life's circumstances, to identify and amplify for clarification existing coping skills and behavioral/cognitive skills including other resources available to you. These are then utilized to facilitate growth and overall improvement in your everyday mode of functioning." The assessment process simply focuses on the situation, your response to the situation, and the available resources that you do possess to cope appropriately and adequately with that situation. It also involves assisting you to view problems in a reality-based attitude (your particular perception of the problem or how you personally define it) and finding a solution suitable to you given your assets and liabilities. Does this information help clarify the process for you?" Jay seemed to acknowledge a basic understanding and Bobby continued. "When we finish the life assessment, I will explain how the process will work individually and specifically for you," he added as if this was a forced or "canned" statement.

Bobby seemed to be pre-occupied with something or someone else but Jay didn't say anything. Jay was very intuitive in this regard because Bobby was pre-occupied with a particular thought. Bobby continued to feel drawn toward Jay in a way he wasn't able to comprehend. Bobby had some formal education (his undergraduate studies when completed would result in a psychology major and a minor in sociology and he had begun to take some of the required Graduate courses) in the counseling field plus specifics he had been taught through his certification requirements and his "self-education" but he had no knowledge of the process called "counter-transference." Each time he had met with Jay, whether formally or informally, a well-fragmented portion of the distant past would emerge. Bobby would continue to be mindful of this phenomenon and discuss this situation with the Program Director after the next scheduled Clinical Staff Meeting.

Bobby went on to explain how an individualized treatment plan would be formulated with Jay's input as well as clinical recommendations from the Treatment Team. This "Treatment Team" concept sparked an interest for Jay. Before Bobby could continue with his monologue, Jay interrupted with a question regarding the Treatment Team. "Bobby, what staff members are included on the treatment team?" Bobby answered, "Well, Jeremy Daniels, the Program Director, Ron Price, the Medical Director, Ross Walker, the Family Program Supervisor, Margaret Doddy, the Nursing Supervisor, Joe McQueen, the Food Services Supervisor, Joyce Little, the Activities Coordinator, Karl Goshin, the Chaplain, and myself, of course." Jay wanted more specifics but that could wait he thought. What degree of power did this team possess? Bobby then said farewell with a reminder regarding the 4:00 P.M. appointment.

Jay watched as Bobby slowly walked toward the Administrative Building. Jay lit another cigarette as others joined him on the front porch of Delta Cottage. Rene was the last to arrive and she sat down beside Jay. Female companionship was the last thing he needed right now and he was in no mood to be sociable. Rene sensed his moodiness and after some small talk joined the other female patients seated near the big oak tree in the front yard.

Rene, with a pronounced purpose to her walk, joined the others assembled at the oak tree. Small talk and chit-chat concerning treatment was the topic of the conversation as Rene approached them. "Well, did you hit on Jay?" Jennifer inquired. "No!" Rene quipped back abruptly. "Why would you ask such a question?" That question did not receive an answer. But the thought occurred to Rene that she would "hit on" Bobby in a second if she had the opportunity to do so. "He doesn't want to talk and he seems to be pre-occupied all the time. I think he's very troubled about something and I think he needs to talk about it." Jennifer was quick to add, "You could be right; maybe he will talk about it during group tomorrow." Jennifer was a schoolteacher who had been caught with a dirty urine screen during a random test mandated by the city school system. She easily discussed these matters in this informal, social gathering but had not really disclosed her problem in the formal group session yet. Mostly she shared superficial, trivial stuff. She was afraid to engage in the therapy process because of her inordinate fears of losing control in front of all those "people." Yes, she was different! "I just smoked a little pot and I had to come to this treatment center," was her reasoning. The others seated around the oak tree listened. Rene finally spoke, "Jennifer, you really need to share this information with the rest of the group members." Jennifer did not answer and choose to remain silent. At this point in her treatment, Jennifer had not developed enough trust to personally disclose a lot of information in the formal setting of the group. To be quite honest, she was afraid the information would get back to the school system and they might fire her. Jennifer was somewhat paranoid about her job because of previous incidents and that was all those people needed were more specifics of her personal life. She would wait. "Well, anyway it's time for supper, let's go," Rene said. All three headed toward the cafeteria with the rest of the group tagging behind them. (Therapy does occur in these types of social groups outside the treatment regimen and WesterBrook purposely reserved additional personal time for just such occasions.)

The assigned counselor attempted to reach his patients where they were in the present and how they reacted to the past with a critical eye on the future: In a word, an exhibition of respect for each patient where dignity and self-growth could be initiated and allowed to flourish. Bobby came to recognize that early in his career as a Counselor that it was necessary for him to understand and to address his patients in terms of their "owned world" because that was the location of whatever freedom they possessed and the freedom they treasured. Little doubt is left to explain the massive walls of denial that is characteristic of the alcoholic or drug addicted individual. The collective patient (the group as a whole) would not be deprived of their "freedom to oblivion" if there was no worthwhile substitute. Bobby felt an obligation in this regard in his individual and group sessions to provide just that "substitute". Bobby also had a deep abiding faith in the inherent potential for change within each patient that was assigned to his caseload. He also had the "knack" in providing situations, especially in the group context, for them to realize this inherent power to change thinking processes and thereby to change behaviors. He had also learned a valuable lesson, in the past however, about assumptions toward his patients and he no longer engaged in that "trap-setting" device. Additionally the importance of meeting the patient on their own "turf," as mentioned earlier, and recognizing the importance of gradual change and the process of allowing the patient to progress slowly to internalize small gains and thus to re-enforce growth. Further, He did not want to set up "failure experiences" for the alcoholic or drug addict that had "failed" in many areas of his life.

The session had been scheduled with Jay for 4:00 P.M. and Bobby was seated in his office chair looking out of his bay window surveying the scene below. Some patients had gathered and were playing volleyball under the supervision of Joyce Little, the Activities Coordinator. Everyone appeared to be having a good time. His surveillance of the scene below was interrupted by a knock on the door. "Come in," Bobby commanded.

Chapter 11 – The Therapeutic Alliance

What Jay would bring to this initial individual session was the primary concern occurring to Bobby as Jay walked into the office. Jay entered the office slowly, shoulders rounded and a bit timid (a little anxious about this encounter?); he didn't bother to close the door behind him (an available escape route, to run-away) or to ask if I wanted it closed; and lastly, he took the chair most removed from me (afraid of closeness, of intimacy?). Here we have three different presentations that must be resolved if this process is to continue and succeed. One concept could handily resolve all three issues: Trust. But that would take time and Bobby knew he did not have the luxury of allowing trust to develop normally and naturally without direct, active intervention on his part. Immediately Bobby thought of the triad that must be overcome if trust is to unfold in the life of the relationship. First, Jay must internalize that he is in no physical, emotional, or psychological danger with his counselor or this process; second, Jay must recognize that consistency in thoughts and predictability in behaviors would prevail throughout the process, and that, third, Jay must also recognize that this was indeed a "helping relationship" where abandonment and other very dedicate issues could be expressed and discussed without fear. For Bobby, "the relationship" was his main concern and that concern had to be communicated clearly to Jay if "engagement" was to occur!

Motivation was another crucial and critical factor to be considered but Bobby was comfortable with the level of motivation exhibited by Jay. Jay had previously verbalized to Bobby a willingness to change, and as his eyes reddened with pain, commented further that he believed he could get the assistance he needed to make the necessary changes in his life at WesterBrook. At the same time, Bobby recognized that motivation is often a fragile, flickering flame that must be fueled by both participants in the dyad to continue to enhance and develop the psychic energy required for change. Bobby would be on the alert to the obvious signs of "low-motivation" or decreasing motivational levels and quickly act to counter them. These signs included the following he recalled: 1. Exhibiting little to no awareness of or insight into the presenting problem; 2. Rarely able to adequately identify problematic situations; 3. An adamant unwillingness to take the risks required for definitive change; and 4. The persistent blaming of others for any misfortunes encountered. These signs and symptoms would absolutely bear watching.

But now to continue with Jay who was attempting to light yet another cigarette. Bobby noticed immediately that Jay appeared to be a "chain-smoker" and this bit of information would be tucked away for future use, if needed. Bobby began by exchanging some small talk with Jay to help ease his apparent intense anxiety and fear. Bobby simply said, "While you are here I will be your assigned Primary Counselor and if you have any concerns or difficulties, bring them to my attention." He continued, "Jay, to make a conscious decision to change and then to follow up with the required actions and behaviors in the process of change is often a journey into the unknown, i.e., to the chaotic, uncharted territory to the uncertain. During your early efforts you will exhibit resistance to change relative to the familiarity of your dysfunction; you will be afraid to abandon old, familiar behaviors and thoughts in favor of new ones! Making the choice to change today means limitations and the real possibility for losses. Limitations on some of your previous personal freedoms and the loss of a long-time friend, alcohol, and that relationship loss requires the completion of a grief process and our spiritual advisor (Chaplain) can help out in that regard. A repetition in various learning devices is required to substantiate and sustain gains made in the action and the decision to change. The choice is there with its attending limitations and potential losses as discussed earlier and many more may unfold as you progress in your recovery efforts. I will, at times, strongly challenge and urge you to cross the "chasm of change."

Jay, it is the way in which you continue to construe or interpret personal circumstances and other events that seems to play the greatest part in the way you feel and subsequently act and react. You will experience change involving mood, behaviors, and cognitions. Other shifts and changes may involve acceptance of normality where previously confusion, chaos, and crisis ruled and dominated your every action and reaction. As you progress in this treatment process, and if you truly want a new way of life, you will acquire a new emerging attitude toward change that is characterized by improved patience and tolerance, flexibility in thinking, healthy skepticism, and openness in your interactions with others and your reactions to others. I am talking about a profound philosophical change toward your feelings, attitudes, and behaviors. Your alcoholic thinking process fought very hard in preventing your acceptance of the serenity that life intended for you. Another subject that must be discussed involves risk-taking behaviors and how you have neglected that area of your life. "Non-risk-taking" and its attending behaviors are deadly consequences to the "psychic-self." This is the fearsome obstacle of the leaving behind of what is and the traveling on to what can be for you. This inability to take the necessary risks in the growth process contributes to your own difficulty and dysfunction. Further, risk-taking behaviors that build a sense of mastery, efficiency, and self-efficacy includes the following: Speaking up instead of holding back, reaching out instead of closing-up, asking for what you want instead of doing without or demanding, trying your best instead of giving up, and taking responsibility and being held accountable instead of blaming others in order for you to find genuine pleasure and satisfaction in the ordinary events of life. It is necessary for you to finally recognize and internalize that your life is no worse than the life of anyone else. Suffering and feeling terrible, now and again, are an acceptable human condition. Jay, I fully realize that I have purposely overloaded you with a great deal of information during this first session. You must begin to internalize the seriousness of your disease! You are not responsible for getting this disease and the experiencing of its many faces; but you, alone, are responsible for your recovery. Your group will hold you accountable daily, one day at a time, and so will I! These handouts will provide some additional material regarding the information I have discussed today with you. Read it and digest it as food for your new life in recovery, if that's the decision you make. Do you have any questions or comments at this time? "

Jay replied, "I will comply with your requests and I'm sure questions will arise." "Good, Bobby said warmly, we'll talk later then."

"Thank you for being on time for our session. One more thing though Jay, I do care about how you progress and I do want to help in any way I can. I will not push or pull but I will walk the distance with you at your side. I hope that in time, with the time you have left in treatment, you'll be able to find me trustworthy: Trust is a necessary component of the therapeutic relationship and "the very foundation upon which your recovery will be based." To aid in that important process, Bobby would continue to present himself as a non-judgmental, concerned, listening helper who would offer to assist Jay in any reasonable way that he might request. And one final comment Bobby interjected: "Remember that other staff members will be meeting with you to complete the various assessments. When those are completed, you and I will meet again and complete the psycho-social assessment and we'll talk about your treatment plan." Jay remarked to

Bobby, "Thank you for your concern and I appreciate your wanting to help me." With that being said Jay left Bobby's office and returned to his cottage to prepare for supper.

Chapter 12 – Into the Group

Shane, the cocaine addict, had been given an assignment by his Primary Counselor and the Clinical Treatment Team to write a "Dear John Letter" to cocaine. Jay normally knew what such a letter implied in real life but to cocaine? Shane was prepared today to read his letter to the group and Jay was actually looking forward to hearing the letter. The counselor prompted Shane to begin. Shane was somewhat hesitant but after fumbling around in his book bag, he came up with the letter neatly folded.

He slowly unfolded the letter and began to read to the hushed group:

"My Dear Lady Cocaine:

For the past nine months you have ruled my life. Your influence and power over me was so strong that at one time I would not have had the strength to write this letter to you. It is time this relationship came to an end. I must admit that we had a great relationship in the beginning. When I was down, you were always there to pick me up or make me happy. When I was tired, I could count on you to help me with renewed energy and vitality. When I felt weak and insecure, you made me feel like a superman. Life with you had been filled with a lot of good times that I'll always remember, yet shared with a lot of bad times that I choose never to forget. There were times when I felt like I'd been up so high that I thought I didn't need anyone but you. And then again, there were times when I felt so low that no one needed me. But, the good times were short, my dear Lady.

Eventually every waking moment I began to think of you. I was obsessed with "your power" and not my own. I was willing to do anything. I never felt alone, but I never felt free. You were always there haunting me, lulling me into trouble, debt, deceit, and adultery. You introduced me to false pride and a bigger than life ego. Dishonesty became a way of living. Lust was a constant companion with us. Guilt was my shadow and shaded everything that we touched. Fantasies became a reality. You are the "big lie." Others told me to watch out for your cunning and powerful ways, but I refused to listen! I knew it all! Your sweet music was the elixir of life and beguiling. You loved using me up and throwing me out into the street to return to you each time as soon as the next paycheck rolled around. There you were with that sick gleam in your eye, beckoning to me. You tried to take my wife and family away from me. You wanted and demanded my very soul. You made me lie and cheat and steal from those who loved me. How come I was so blind, how come I couldn't say no to your insane ideas? You had me in your grasp and you wouldn't allow me to be free. You absolutely controlled me with your illicit charms.

But suddenly somehow, something happened! A power greater than you'll ever be, has entered my life. And this power showed me the way out of this deadly relationship. I know now what I need to do to keep you at a distance. I know you will never go away, but now I have hope and friends and Narcotics Anonymous. It doesn't cost me $200.00 a night to talk with my Higher Power or go to my meetings. It doesn't cost me my self-esteem and self-confidence or invoke those intense feelings of shame, guilt, and horrifying remorse. Your alter-ego, Paranoia, doesn't guide me today through your jealous rages. You see, my new friends don't want me to use, they don't want me to lose my family and they certainly don't want me to die! So this is how it ends. Our affair of passion and poison is over because you have hurt me long enough. I have no regrets because today, I can accept myself just as I am and I have no desire to return to your deadly arms. Another thing, I know that I have to stay away from your family too and that includes alcohol, other sedatives, narcotics, and all the rest of your relatives. They're too close to you and if I spend time with them, I will be right back to you again. I wanted to make this a "clean" break but I know you all too well to expect that to happen. I know that you'll always be there, just waiting for me to forget. I will not forget that you are very persistent and extremely possessive! My address and telephone are listed under another lover's name but that is my secret.

Rest in Peace!"

The hush continued in the group room and as Jay glanced around, he could see group members trying to hide the tears that persistently wanted to be released. The group sat silently and motionless allowing the full impact of what they had just heard sink into their addictive minds. At last, Shane spoke and talked of the difficulty that he had experienced in writing that letter. He further added that as he was thinking about the assignment, he knew that when he had finished it, so would his illicit affair with cocaine end. Deep down inside, he knew that now. He sat there in his hurt and pain and softly cried as never before. Indeed he wanted this love affair to be over and his grief bore that out specifically. Shane said sheepishly, "This recovery thing really frightens me but when I think of the past and the dreadful experiences with my cocaine 'runs', I really get scared! I have lost so much to cocaine; will I ever be able to regain what I have lost?" Shane said. All of the group members offered him encouragement and support and even Bobby and Janice joined in with their support. Bobby spoke up about the losses Shane referred to and said that the grief process must be completed prior to a committed life of sobriety. And Shane, for the first time, freely accepted what Bobby had said. Bobby and Janice complimented Shane on the good job with his assignment and thanked him for allowing the group to learn more about him.

Jay could not contain the question that on his mind. "Bobby," he said, "What is this grief thing you're talking about?" Jay tentatively inquired. "In a few simple words, Jay, it's recognizing your ability to move beyond the losses you have experienced whether they are past, present, and future. Grief can be defined as a normal and natural response to loss. There are five rather specific stages in the grief process and they are: gaining awareness, accepting responsibility, identifying communications, taking action, and moving beyond the losses. Additionally, other clinicians recognize five stages that closely parallel the above and they are: Denial, anger, depression, bargaining, and acceptance. Each stage must be resolved; there is no skipping around, no short-cuts. Our chaplain can help you with these stages and the process of moving beyond your losses. For now, suffice it to say that the process does exist and assistance is available to you. In a way, we're taught how to acquire things but not how to lose them."

Jay sat there; taking all of this in, wondering what it must have been like to be as obsessed with such a powerful drug as cocaine! Jay's denial was again in high gear working overtime because he refused to consciously consider the obsessive feature of his own use of alcohol. He would give that idea some thought later. His anxiety began to rise without warning and this concerned him. "Am I afraid of this group process?" he wondered. "Maybe," he thought.

Bobby then urged the group to consider various feelings and then discuss how others can color emotions (feelings) and reactions. Bobby inquired, "David, how did that previous interaction feel?" David responded, "Cold and distant." Janet then inquired, "Do you mean that cold and distant are feelings?" Bobby then responded, "Good comment, Janet. David, can you tell us more to help Janet understand?" David explained thusly, "Cold not as a temperature but as an emotional temperature, distant, not physically close, but at an emotional distance (far away, not approachable!)." Bobby commented, "Does that help, Janet?" "Yes, it is much clearer now." Janet then asked David what caused him to experience that encounter as cold and distant. "Well, I was talking with Shane and I asked if he would like to go for coffee and he just seemed cold and distant in his reply to me," David offered. Janet continued to push David, "What seemed cold and distant?" Bobby interjected quickly and professionally, "Easy as we explore this train of thought and of feelings. Continue David if you wish." David did continue, "I've known him for years and I guess that I expected a more cordial response." Janet again pushed the issue and said, "So your expectations were unfulfilled, you were disappointed. Is that right?" Bobby being very protective of the group and its dynamics offered, "Janet, careful, your thoughts and feelings only." David countered, "No, not really disappointed! But the negative interaction and the response did a number on my self-esteem. It seems that other's response to me must be in the most positive light or else I feel 'less than'. Does that make any sense to you?" Others chimed into the conversation in unison with a resounding 'yes'! Bobby then stated, "All seek affirmation (approval) in day-to-day living to some degree, but if others 'put you down', you may feel 'less than'. Continued negative assaults to the psyche can give rise to self-loathing! In this regard you may begin actively seeking affirmations (approval) from everyone and that's a difficult road to travel and it will ruin your day! This has been a great exchange and thanks for allowing me to participate and to see that group continues to give hope, strength, and recovery. This has clearly defined the group process for us today." Bobby then closed the meeting for the morning.

It was break time and time for a cigarette before lunch and then the lectures and workshops afterwards. The other group members continued to talk with Shane, hugging his neck, and there were more tears and warm words expressed. That cigarette is calling to me Jay remarked to himself and out the door he headed. The rest of the day involved lunch and the didactic presentations and Jay was getting tired after the heavy group session in the morning. He was anxious to call a halt to this day and put it behind him. He finally returned to cottage Delta after eating and prepared for the 8:00 P.M. Alcoholics Anonymous meeting. By 9:30 P.M. he was preparing to get into bed for the sleep he felt he truly deserved. He put his clothes away and climbed into his bed. As he lay there his mind replayed the day's events as the stream outside slowly invited sleep.

Chapter 13 - And Group Continues

Bobby sat upright in his chair after formally opening the group session and remarked, "It is truly remarkable how many people on a day-to-day basis walk around in fears, of others, of life in general, and even of themselves. Today each of you will confront your particular fear, your "bogey-man". The other group members looked somewhat confused as they looked for validation in each other's eyes. "What was he talking about," they collectively thought. No one spoke as Bobby continued. Consciously, fears and anxiety serve to protect you to insure your very survival. At a deeper level they serve to methodically "slay" you. They stay locked inside and slowly eat their way out! At this deeper level, your comprehension is dreamy (no problems here) and the pressures of everyday occurrences do not or dare not enter. These are reserved for the night with terrifying, fitful dreams that are chaotic bordering on the bizarre. You do not have ready access to this region allowing you to discharge the stored negative energy thereby actively dealing with those fears and anxieties." Jay pondered that statement and realized that for him, it was true. Bobby continued. "With that being said, each of you will take one of these cards, and write your most dreaded fear upon it. Do not sign your name and return the cards to me. Take ten minutes now and complete this assignment."

Now the group felt as tight as if they were snails and someone had dumped a box of salt onto them. Some finished rather quickly but others seemed to be laboring with the assignment. Jay sat still and gazed at the white card in front of him. His attention was diverted to the past when Kayce would accuse him of being non-feeling. He had always thought that feelings had to be controlled and being out of control was the worst possible situation. He easily exaggerated situations and he was an expert at playing the extreme positions. He was always comfortable at either extreme and knew nothing about compromise, black or white, never the prospect of gray!

His anxiety was rising as the thought of this assignment consumed him. Ten minutes to identify and write down on a white card his "most dreaded fear." This statement had caused an internal shift at the emotional and cognitive level. Extremists in philosophical situations and discussions tended to gather at the point most comfortable and most familiar to them. Jay fit that description perfectly. His negativity of spirit brightly glowed daily. His first thought was to write down "fears in general" with the intellectual thought that would be safe. Everyone has fears, so what if they felt he was being dishonest with himself and with others." As well as he could recollect, fears of every description had haunted him for as long as he could remember. The fear of not measuring up to his father, "his impeccable father", of not pleasing those that he knew he must please, the fear of appearing foolish in front of others, the fear of his other class-mates), the fear of being found lacking in some aspect of his life, the fear of winning or losing, and the fear of success or failure. His life had been predicated upon these fears and more. They repeatedly motivated him to seek relief and oblivion through the "assured" effects of alcohol.

His life was filled with "musts, oughts, shoulds, and can'ts" (Albert Ellis). Self-defeating attitudes and behaviors permeated his very existence. He had never considered the degree of stress he typically carried around in his day-to-day affairs. Anxiety was a sense of dread for him but he could never validate for himself the specific cause of his varying degrees of anxiety. He had read a book about "anxiety" and the definition provided didn't seem to fit what he felt: "Anxiety is the fear of being hurt or of losing something."

He simply dreaded the feeling that arose each time and it scared him. He made the decision.

He picked up the white card and began to print the word! "Hey Jay, wake up, it's time for breakfast," his room-mate called out to him. Jay slowly opened his eyes and looked toward Howard. Jay's eyes were wide now and they expressed a certain relief that, indeed, it was time for breakfast. The dream had caused him to begin to think more and rationalize less, to being more aware, that indeed, it was time to recognize that he had some difficulties and they "demanded resolution". He slowly got out of bed and headed for the shower. He told Howard to go on to breakfast without him and he would be right behind him. Jay stood in the shower with the warm invigorating water cascading down upon him. He leaned on the shower stall and as quietly as an unborn baby's tear began to cry softly. Almost immediately a sense of warmness and a glow enveloped and surrounded him as if someone had turned on a heat lamp in the shower that bathed him with a calmness that he had never felt before. Was he having a "break-down" or something? He didn't understand and curiously his "non-understanding" did not seem to bother him that much. Something had happened and he wanted very much to sustain the feeling.

Jay completed the shower and dressed hurriedly because he did not want to miss breakfast nor the peer community meeting that was scheduled each morning. Something new stirred the community on a daily basis and today would prove to be no different. As he walked out of the cottage, he noticed that Rene had just stepped out of the cottage next door and was headed in his direction. "I suppose she wants to walk to the cafeteria with me," Jay thought to himself. He gave her a smile and a wave as she approached. Both exchanged small-talk as they continued to breakfast. As they entered the cafeteria-style line, several of the group members turned to look but said nothing with a smirking grim on their face. Jay chose to overlook the glances and proceeded to get his tray and sat down with Howard and the rest of the group to eat. They were about finished with their meals but they seemed to be waiting for some kind of comment from Jay. He did not give them what they wanted and soon each in turn began to leave the table to dump their trays. Howard was the last to leave and even he gave Jay a peculiar smile as he departed.

What are they thinking? Jay thought. Do they think we had sex before breakfast or something? He would make an effort to deal with these misperceptions, misunderstandings or accusations during the group session. Jay got up and dumped his tray and headed toward the community meeting room. Jay was beginning to look forward to the day's events because each day he learned something new. And for Jay, the learning he was experiencing would prove to be critical post-discharge. The Mayor of the community called the meeting to order as Jay took a seat next to Howard. (This meeting was always conducted in an informal group format with everyone sitting in a huge circle.) Several administrative-type announcements were made and then any peer-related issues were brought up for discussion. Nearly every morning all clinical staff members were present. This gave immediate access to staff that could respond. This was not meant to be a gripe session and normally it served the function of getting the day's activities off to a positive, upbeat start. All eyes were directed toward Jay after the administrative announcements were read. "Well, I guess this is a good time to clear the air," he said to himself. But what to say troubled him! He decided to simply say that he slept late and nearly missed breakfast and it wouldn't happen again. The group seemed to express approval with the simple truth and that was that. Funny though, Rene glanced over toward Jay and smiled. "What was that about," Jay wondered. The community group was closed by the Mayor and Jay headed for the patio for a much needed cigarette prior to the 9:15 A.M. group session.

As he walked toward the patio, Bobby motioned to Jay. "Jay, I have scheduled another individual session with you for 4:15 P.M. today to do some treatment planning and discuss the various assessments that have been completed." "Right, I'll be there," Jay replied.

Chapter 14 – With the Therapist Again!

The clock struck 4:00 P.M. as Bobby sat in his office, leaning back in his over-stuffed desk chair getting prepared for his session at 4:15 P.M. with Jay. With the information gathered thus far and the invested time in the therapeutic relationship, Bobby was now prepared to discuss with Jay the findings as a result of all the various assessments; the Clinical Team referred to it as a biopsychosocial diagnostic summation. But he wondered what truly motivated Jay and at various times, his "miraculous recovery" status scared him. Jay was exhibiting a strong need to be unconditionally accepted and continued to present in the best possible light except for occasional emotional outbursts. It is true that Jay needed structure, consistency, guidance, and "reality-predictability" in his recovery because people in general, and specifically dependency-prone individuals, find randomness and uncertainty extremely aversive. Given the lack of parental emotional engagement and the strongly exhibited need to be accepted unconditionally, the alcoholic or drug addict as a population, is driven (compelled) to seek inordinate status, power, and influence. The individual is driven to seek outside himself the validation of his own existence. This continued seeking from the outside what can only be furnished from the inside leads to constant frustration and despair; i.e., in short order they began to perceive themselves as empty and deprived. This then leads to an ingrained perception that others are rejecting and this ideation leads to resentments. The individual becomes a resentful, angry, and disappointed person. Is it any wonder that alcohol and other addictive substances become their sole mistress and only friend? Isolation becomes a "coping skill" and as discussed previously a hostile view of the world may well emerge. The inability to soothe and calm the "self" is instrumental in setting up self-destructive behaviors and self-defeating attitudes continuing to place the individual constantly in destructive and painful circumstances, situations, and relationships.

Jay's well constructed "miraculous recovery" defense system could be attributable to his own ingrained suspicious and hostile nature (albeit, covert, most of the time). His internalized defended decision to sublimate his basic suspiciousness and volatile, hostile manner was not due to the shortage of available help from the group or from me but in the past those two elements were the roadblocks resulting in his perceived emotional starvation and deprivation; his inability to establish and maintain healthy, long lasting interpersonal relationships. When the individual begins to question his own capacity to mean anything to anyone, frustration becomes despair leading the alcoholic and/or drug addict to perceive that he lacks the ability to make a difference in another person's life. He feels unloved and unwanted at a most primitive level of existence. He cannot enjoy life's simple pleasures without his resorting to his chemical catalyst. Even Jay's inordinate desire to please his parents through "accomplishments" had been unproductive. Research and experience within this field of addictions reveals that dysfunctional (alcoholic) parents normally preclude any recognition, much less consistent support of their children's academic, athletic, or artistic achievements. For them to expect anything good to happen, like a nice birthday party, family outing to the zoo, attending a sporting event, or a holiday becomes a foolish desire since it would either be forgotten or, if it took place at all, ruined by negative behaviors and possibly violent behaviors; i.e., one or both of the parents would be drunk. Jay's recounted familial history validated addiction in at least one of the family members, possibly the mother and maybe the father. The grandfather's history was well defended and maybe he was alcoholic also. It is any wonder that Jay grew up being perfectionist and negativistic (suspicious and hostile) given his early home environment. However, it's not "nature or nurture," per se, that determines the intrinsic flavor of the person's basic attitudes and behaviors. It is the internalized, conceptualized responses to various situations that dictates the outcomes and gives rise to self-defeating behaviors and attitudes. And if these remain unchecked, an extremely hostile view of the world can emerge. Given his pre-disposition to addiction, it is absolutely predictable that Jay responded as he did to "self," to others, and to the outside world that he called "his life consumed with alcohol." He simply responded as he had been "programmed" to respond. All of the above contributed to a reduction in Jay's self-esteem or possibly as a block to his emerging "self"; the way he perceived himself as a result of other's appraisals. These beliefs toward the "self-system" are internalized in the maturational process via attitudes that others reflected back to Jay, such as those values presented by his parents (whether re-enforced or not), peers ("chums," classmates), and significant others (teachers, preachers/priests, girlfriends). These combine to determine the self-worth, the self-system, the value, that Jay has for himself; i.e., what am I worth today?

Bobby continued to ruminate through the various assessment instruments within his mind's eye to ferret out other roadblocks to Jay's recovery. Three issues surfaced for Bobby that required extensive work by Jay and they were all tied to his "self-system": 1. the fear of self-disclosure, 2. the fear of rejection, and 3. a generalized anxiety syndrome that is exacerbated by the first two concerns. Group therapy in combination with didactic presentations coupled with individual sessions to deal with these three issues would comprise his counseling treatment plan. Specific cognitive restructuring would alleviate much of the anxiety and within the process Jay would gain a better acceptance of "self" and a reduction of the fears that drove him deeper into personal and social oblivion through his continued use of alcohol.

Bobby would assist Jay in the process of identifying and altering his irrational beliefs and negative self-statements and thoughts. Bobby recognized clearly that Jay's anxiety-related situations were the direct result of his well-entrenched and defended irrational thought system. Verbal persuasion, teaching, and identifying negative talk would be the primary tools utilized in assisting Jay to dispute his irrational belief system.

Bobby's antique clock began to chime indicating 4:15 P.M. He amusingly expected Jay to suddenly materialize in front of his desk as the clock sounded the last note, but instead a knock at the door. Bobby got up and walked slowly to the door. Jay stood there waiting as if he expected to be invited to enter. Bobby turned slightly to one side as he prompted Jay to enter. Bobby purposefully added another chair to his office giving Jay a choice to sit near him or to take a more distant seat. Jay took the chair near Bobby. Jay's unconscious decision to choose the chair nearest Bobby was an indication of his budding trust in the relationship and that pleased Bobby. "How are you doing today?" Bobby inquired. "Oh, my feelings are somewhat better but physically, I feel great," Jay responded. "Today we will discuss your treatment plan that will deal specifically with three issues of fear of self-disclosure, fear of rejection, and generalized anxiety." Bobby had contemplated on how to approach Jay about reaching out for help and his generalized anxiety as a direct result. He wanted Jay to know it was quite normal to admit the need for help no matter how strange or ridiculous it might seem to others. He recalled an episode from the Mary Tyler Moore Show. That would work!

He would relate the story to Jay. "Are you familiar with the old television series called the Mary Tyler Moore Show?" "Yes," Jay responded. "Well, Ted Baxter, the news anchorman, was experiencing problems which led his wife to insist that Ted see a psychiatrist. Ted was embarrassed to go alone and insisted Lou Grant, his boss, accompany him. As they were sitting in the doctor's reception area, Ted shared a recurring dream with Lou." (Perhaps the dream would cause a chuckle and Jay would lighten up about reaching out for help and reduce his anxiety levels.) Bobby chuckled as he remembered the situation. "Ted told Lou: 'I dreamed I was in a large group of people and some kangaroos were there also. There was also a duck present. He never said anything. I don't know why he was there! Anyway, the people and kangaroos were talking and milling about. This one kangaroo comes up to me and asks me who I am. I tell him I'm Ted Baxter, the news anchorman. The kangaroo says no, I can't be because he's Ted Baxter, news anchorman. We begin to argue and soon everyone is beginning to get involved. The kangaroo finally says "I can prove I am Ted Baxter," and reaches into his pouch and pulls out a business card and hands it to me. I look at it and it says, "Ted Baxter, News Anchorman." So I reach into my pocket and pull out my business card. Lou is looking at Ted, "Well, Ted, what does your card say?" "Bucky, the Kangaroo," Ted exclaims. At this point, everyone including the kangaroos begin to leave, all except the duck. He just waddles over and disgraces himself on my shoe." "What does it all mean, Lou? Am I doing the right thing in being here?" Lou looks at Ted and with very little facial expression says, "You are doing the right thing Ted and the duck did too!" Jay sat there and his laughter combined with Bobby's laughter filled the room. Both men had a hearty laugh with this story and Jay did feel better!

Bobby had handled this very sensitive matter in a profoundly professional manner and the intervention was successful.

Bobby then went on to explain in detail the remaining issues that had surfaced and explained the specifics of the treatment plan, itself, and what he expected Jay to do. Bobby knew this treatment plan was tentative, at best. He considered it a departure point to guide future treatment. As Jay progressed and other information was gathered, other issues identified, or the occurrence of a significant event, the treatment plan could easily be revised or discarded. It was not written in "stone." The treatment plan was meant to drive the process of change, not to smother it or to be so inflexible that it allowed little deviation. This type of treatment was sometimes referred to as "cookie cutter" treatment where everyone received the same doses of the same treatment. Bobby knew individuals needed "individualized" care and that was the philosophy he carried into all of his patient relationships. He would explain all of this in detail to Jay at the appropriate time.

He also took this opportunity to introduce Jay to the self-help philosophy and Alcoholics Anonymous. AA meetings were held nightly and Jay was expected to attend on a regular basis, as part of his treatment plan.

Further, he asked Jay if he had any specific concerns that were causing him distress that he wanted to work within the group. Bobby was eliciting Jay's input into the treatment plan itself with this question. Jay responded with an indication that he would have his hands full with what they had just discussed. But he did have a question regarding this "belief system thing." Jay remarked, "I can begin to understand and appreciate the degree of severity involved in a strictly irrational set of beliefs but I am having difficulty gaining a perspective on the "disputing"' part of the restructuring process. Can you explain that to me in some detail?" "First Jay, Bobby said, the situation is reviewed thoroughly. You do not get into a hurry with this step for suddenly the magical or negative belief system associated with the particular situation will readily emerge (the "self-defeating statement") to be followed by an emphatic transition statement (a "bridge-type statement") and closed with a positive "self-enhancing" statement. Jay responded enthusiastically to Bobby's precise explanation. "I can do that!" Jay responded eagerly.

Bobby then revealed to Jay that no medical problems were noted that could hinder his recovery efforts. His dietary supplement would resolve his weight gain and replenish his vitamin deficiency. Spiritual aspects were already being addressed and your responses to the interventions have been favorable. I am concerned about your "honey-moon" attitude with your treatment. There are some hard issues that will emerge as you progress with your treatment plan and I want you to know explicitly that I support your efforts. Bobby was attempting to reiterate his previous "wanting to help" attitude and to further enhance Jay's faith in the process of treatment and in the process of recovering. Bobby further decided to take this opportunity to explore with Jay the concept of "change" and change contracting.

Bobby said, "Jay, I want to reveal some hard questions for you and careful with your internalized replies, because in the answering of these questions and your attitude toward them, you will learn to take direct and personal responsibility for your own well-being. Are you ready?" Jay replied, "Yes." "What do you want to be different in your life? What behaviors are you willing to overcome in order that the desired level of functioning might occur? Which parts of you would you be willing to assist you in this endeavor and which parts of you might try to sabotage these efforts to change? How can you practice these behavioral changes within the context of the group process? What can the group do to assist you in this endeavor? Can you generalize what is internalized within the group to the outside world? Are you willing?" Jay's facial expression changed as he tried to absorb these "hard questions" as presented by Bobby. "You are right, Bobby, those are elegant existential questions, and I will write them down and review them very carefully." "It's not necessary for you to do that Jay. Here is a typed copy of them. Remember that attitude is important in this process of looking at your 'self' and your motivation. "And within the context of change, Jay, you must begin to methodically develop a cooperative, confident, and determined attitude and spirit toward your life of recovery," Bobby urged. "Begin the process of 'adoption'; i.e., adopting and adapting to your new life of recovery and sobriety. The moving beyond a life scarred and marred by the disease of alcoholism filled by a desperate obsession and compulsion to a life of resiliency and the engrained desire to survive. Cradle and care for it as you would nurture a newborn; i.e., provide guidance, consistency, and room to grow and nourish it gently to sustain growth."

Bobby used this opportunity to further instill Jay's continuing motivation by using a bit of humor that would be attractive to his right-brain processing. Bobby said, "Jay, how many counselors does it take to change a light bulb?"(Author unknown) Jay knew he was being set up for the joke (and that's exactly how his left-brain responded!) and offered, "Well, two, maybe three." "Wrong," Bobby countered, "it takes only one, but the light bulb's gotta really wanta change!" Jay laughed heartily. Bobby knew and intuitively sensed when to encourage, confront, and to influence. In this metaphor, he was attempting, in a subtle way, to influence Jay by trying to circumvent Jay's propensity to extreme intellectualizations (intellectualizing is the absolute refusal to deal with feelings regarding a given situation and choosing to direct his primary attention processing only to the behavioral aspect of the situation).

His suspicious nature would be a difficult defect to resolve. Jay's overall attitude needed an adjustment and recognizing that attitudes are more important than factual evidence, Bobby's plan was to make suggestions directly to Jay's unconscious "self" via the right-brain, thereby making a breakthrough possible. Beyond any doubt, Jay's grandiose and self-centered core coupled with his feelings of unworthiness had concretized his defensive facade of patronizing and people-pleasing coping skills in combating his feelings of fragmentation and incompleteness. To further attack Jay's massive defensive system, another metaphor would be utilized.

"Jay, are you familiar with the Star Trek series of television fame?" "Yes," Jay responded, somewhat puzzled. "When Captain Kirk orders the *shields* to be raised, what is happening?" "Well, I suppose that he is trying to prevent damage to his ship by the Klingons or other enemies." "That is correct Jay, Bobby offered affirmatively; when something or someone gets too close, the defenses go on full alert." Jay continued to look somewhat puzzled at this story but Bobby knew the strategy would be successful because his right-brain had grasped the metaphor and it would allow the "truth of the metaphor" to emerge gracefully. The shields required tremendous amounts of energy to sustain hit after hit and with each hit, energy was absorbed and utilized; i.e., energy the starship needed to sustain life and ensure survival. (It was unfortunate that the advanced technology, of the era portrayed, did not provide a mechanism of re-cycling or re-capturing the energy created by a direct hit from an outside source thereby setting up a sort of self-perpetuating source of energy with no chance of a shortage.) A great deal of time and emotional energy is invested and expended by the dependent person in maintaining his defensive and denial systems (his protective shields). Extreme care must be taken by the counselor in attacking those closely held systems through inappropriate confrontations, especially within the group context. This was the explicit message implied in the metaphor and Bobby continued to be comfortable with the impact it would have on Jay's psychic "self." His unconscious "self" would begin to assimilate the "implied message." Jay then commented, "I didn't know you identified with those 'Trekkie' fans." "Oh, yeah, I have most of the episodes on video cassettes. The series was somewhat before its time, but some of the episodes were a little too far out for me, though."

With that, Bobby escorted Jay to the door and returned to his desk. "Elegant existential questions were they?" Bobby chuckled to himself as he sank down into his favorite leather chair. Those "elegant existential questions" would haunt Jay and furnish him nights of tossing and turning because they were postulated for Jay's "unconscious self" and his right brain formulations would work overtime to dispel his intellectualizations sustained by his left-brain thinking. Bobby assessed Jay to be a rather independent person but, somehow, he had to guide Jay to internalize that to be truly independent was not only to recognize his own strengths and weakness but also to gain awareness of his interdependence upon others. Bobby hoped that Jay could continue to be enthusiastic and eager maintaining his motivational levels and the psychic energy required to sustain that motivation.

Bobby closed his eyes and gently repeated the "Serenity Prayer" looking forward to his next scheduled appointment. His next scheduled session was set for 2:00 P.M. and presently it was 1:15 P.M. Bobby chose this time to consider the situation that had emerged with Rene. Yes, she was an absolutely attractive young woman and the combination of her requests for an inordinate number of individual sessions, her continued attempts to gain my attention, and more recently, her seductive behavioral displays concerns me. My supervision visit with the Program Director explained and clarified the concepts of transference and counter-transference and now I was experiencing a firsthand account of those transference dynamics at work within Rene. A couple of choices were available in handling this situation and it must be dealt with immediately. First, within the group process, I could talk directly to Rene and disclose the concerns or secondly, Janice could explore sexual attractiveness or personal relationships within the group and through vicarious learning help Rene recognize the dynamics involved. Allowing Rene to continue and to potentially act upon her transference was not an option. The intervention must be devised and acted upon. He would discuss the situation in the morning with Janice and plan strategies accordingly. His professional conduct and ethics precluded any type of relationship with a patient. He must be above reproach with his interactions with all patients entrusted to his care. Further, he was aware of the emotional vulnerability existing within Rene and in all such cases a professional stance was mandated.

Chapter 15 - And More Group

"Jay, I think it is great that you could see Rene's sadness from her facial expression and the way she was talking; I know it helped Rene and others be more aware of their own feelings in this situation and like situations, and it helped Rene to begin the process of trusting her own feelings to others and to talk about what's really going on with her." "Rene thanks for sharing those hurtful feelings with us. In the past you tended to hold those feelings inside resulting in escalating needs for expression. They demanded expression and you went straight to the medicine cabinet to self-medicate them. You are growing in your ability to cope with those buried feelings." Bobby further commented that feelings that emerge which are painful might get worse before they improve. This comment from the Counselor scared Rene and she reacted defensively and stated, "That's easy for you to say. I'm the one who feels terrible and now I'm being singled out to dissect my feelings." Bobby tried to soothe her ruffled feathers. "Feelings are neither good nor bad, they just are," he said. "You will all experience difficulties expressing your feelings and being 'real' with each other. The use of addictive substances numbs you to your various feelings states but as you clear and progress in your personal growth here at WesterBrook, expressing, owning and discussing feelings will come easier for you. No pain, no gain!" Hell, which was easy for him to say, Jay silently remarked to himself. Bobby then asked if anyone wanted to share. Jennifer sat quietly and wondered why Bobby kept glancing toward her as if he was giving her explicit permission to join the conversation.

Finally he said, "Jennifer, do you have a comment you'd like to make?" Jennifer replied hesitantly, "I'm a user of marijuana only. I don't drink beer or whiskey but occasionally I'll have a glass of wine for dinner. I'm afraid that the City School System now has what they needed to fire me." Jay then shared that he could understand Jennifer's concern about her job. He might be in the same situation himself. However he offered some advice regarding Federal and State Laws and the City's own drug-free program and rather specific policies. With Jay's remarks, Jennifer began to exhibit a real fear bordering on paranoia and told Jay she didn't ask for his advice and in the future keep his legalese crap to himself! Secretly she felt extremely paranoid about the information she had received. The other peers seemed to approve of what Jay had said and the way he offered the information to her by chastising Jennifer in her negative reactions. Perhaps she could find the courage to be more open and receptive to the group and share with them at a more intimate level. Her mother had told her repeatedly to "never air your dirty laundry in public!" That admonition stayed with her. Jennifer recalled her difficulties with "girl-talk" finding it difficult even then to talk about things that really upset her. Even her best friend knew nothing that was really significant about her, only superficial, trivial things. With the possible support and encouragement of the group, perhaps it would be possible to trust this group. She would try. She thought of the things she said to Jay, or more aptly, fired toward Jay. "Why did I attack him that way?" Bobby wondered silently why Jennifer would seem to request help from the group and then as quickly discount what they had offered to her. Bobby commented to himself that he must be even more attentive to this particular group of patients and endeavor to listen for the obvious in their interactional communications.

This, indeed, was a challenging caseload. After the internal monologue, Jennifer explained to the group her hesitation mixed with anxiety and before she realized it, the past emerged in words that seem to bring relief with every syllable. Afterwards she felt better and the paranoid feelings began to slowly slip away. The group offered continued support and praise for her honesty and the way she allowed the group to share in the hurts and disappointments of her life. Jay had left behind his "advice-giving" and began to self-consciously recall past experiences of some of his own hurts as a result of his alcoholism. What the woman said made sense to him and strangely enough gave him the courage to probe his deeper fears and frustrations. He again thought of Shelby, the relationship with her and the relationship with Kayce. What was he looking for in these relationships? Why did he find it almost normal for him to be with Shelby and married to Kayce? Jay was oblivious to Bobby's voice.

"Jay, where are you?" he requested again. Jay lifted his head and the energy went out of his eyes. Bobby did not speak allowing Jay to lead the way. Jay's hands were clammy and he rubbed his palms against his pants as if in the drying of them, he could wipe away the disturbing thoughts that possessed him. He was searching for the words but they would not come. He looked at Bobby and shook his head hoping that Bobby would understand that he had not found the key to release them. Shane, seated next to Jay, reached over and touched his hand lightly offering unsolicited support and encouragement. Bobby still did not intervene. Jay had to cross the "chasm alone" and he had to find the courage to risk from within to make the "leap of faith" to truly begin the journey. Group time was running out but still Bobby sat in silence. Jay, after two or three anxiety, laden minutes began to make the choice, .however awkward, he would try. He reminded himself that he felt secure in this group. Sure he was anxious about this but he felt no outside pressure to perform. A thought intruded: Would the group continue to be as supportive when his facade crumbled? Despite his uncertainty, he tentatively began to tell his story; the story that needed to be told.

Jay spoke softly as he began to tell his story. The group was attentive yet encouragingly supportive. He related to them his earliest recollections of drinking alcohol and what a very grown up thing to do or so he felt. At eleven years old, he yearned to be an adult more so than any other child of eleven. Time wouldn't pass quickly enough for him. He was so preoccupied with the future that time in the present had no relevance. He felt as if to be a child was to be set adrift destined to aimlessly wander into the infinite. He grew up very quickly with some calling him "precocious" among other names. The group laughed at that remark. Jay continued. "I never really felt I belonged. I even had fantasies that I was adopted and my parents were not my real parents. I suppose the feelings arose because my father seemed so distant. Looking back, my father was very devoted to my mother and at times doted on her. At times I have felt anger and resentment toward my mother for robbing me of the relationship I deserved. Our relationship, at best, was adversarial in nature. I have never discussed this with anyone before and never would consider talking with my mother about it. I want to be relieved of this discomfort but not at the expense of my mother. I was never satisfied with just being "me"; a normal eleven year old kid who got into all manner of mischief. I learned early how to manipulate others to get my needs and wants met. "Everything" was never enough! I recall being taught how to acquire things, being told that winning was the most important outcome, and to always strive for excellence (even at the expense of others) and accumulate wealth. I was never taught how to live or to be able to answer to myself the simplest of life's questions. I was never taught how to lose, to graciously lose, to recognize the loss, to accept it, and to move on with my life. I seemed to always feel more deeply about various situations especially so if someone criticized my actions. I had to please others. But I also knew that manipulation was required in the "pleasing process." There was always a secondary gain to be had. I recall only one close friend, Jon, who remains my best friend today. Not because I did anything to cultivate it. Jon is special and always will be. I'm glad I can call him my friend." Tears slowly rolled down Jay's cheeks. He continued. "This is so very difficult for me. I have hurt so many people in my life. I haven't told you about Shelby. She's another special person that I have used and abused. My wife continues to have faith in me but I am afraid the love we once had is gone." By this time he was sobbing openly and abruptly ended his story.

The group sat in silence with Jay still sobbing. Howard touched his hand with encouragement. Silence again. At long last Bobby said, "Jay you did better than I thought you would. Your honesty and feelings are real and the tears are real. Look around this group and see the face of honesty. It appears to me that you are beginning the process of trusting yourself and others with your feelings. This trusting attitude combined with your exhibited ability today to take risks will result in a new view of yourself. Jay within the depths of your story, I believe you have answered "yes" to the three most important questions all alcoholics and/or drug addicts must ask themselves: Am I alcoholic or drug addicted? (Recognition of the diseased condition), Am I defeated? (Admission of need for help), and, is it Okay today? (Acceptance). I am proud of you. Thank you for your sharing today. This is a good time to break for today.

"Howard, begin the Serenity Prayer for us." As the others left the group room, Jay remained seated. He continued to feel his pain that he had always soothed with alcohol. Bobby walked over to him, touched his shoulder, and said, "Today you felt the pain without alcohol and you have talked about the pain without alcohol. That's real growth, Jay." Jay looked up at the man he did not know until days ago and said, "Thanks." Bobby walked out of the room without responding but he did turn and smile at Jay. Jay needed a cigarette and in a strange way he felt embarrassment. Where had he learned to experience guilt as a result of being honest with his feelings? He remembered the words of the poster in Bobby's office: "Some days, the dragon wins". That seemed to be appropriate.

Chapter 16 - And Treatment Continues

Those feelings that surfaced during group continued to haunt Jay with instant replays in his mind. His sleep was fitful and he awoke this morning with the feeling he had been drinking all night. He felt as if he had a terrible hangover and he knew what that felt like. He had been up since 5:00 A.M. and had already smoked several cigarettes and consumed at least five cups of coffee. "Thought-stopping" refused to work for him this time. Within his consciousness he wanted to be free of those negative feelings. They felt so "fresh," so real, as if it was yesterday. Shane walked out onto the patio and said good morning to him. Jay responded slowly. Shane recognized a hangover when he saw one, "Bad night, huh?" Jay simply said, "Yes." As the morning wore on toward Group, Jay was anxious about being confronted in the group about his discomfort. If Shane recognized his discomfort, then certainly the group would and if not, Bobby would absolutely! As the group assembled and moved into the group room, a hush quickly settled over the environment. The group began as scheduled. Bobby spoke briefly followed by some announcements from Janice. As they spoke, Jay grew more anxious. His palms were sweating, his heart was racing, warmth engulfed him, and he felt nauseated. Bobby then looked directly at Jay.

"Here it comes; Jay thought and braced himself as best he could. He couldn't lose control, not now!" "Jay, I keep thinking about group yesterday. You brought up some very sensitive material that is referred to as "unfinished business" and you should think about beginning the process of "closure." It is important that you reach a compromise with those feelings of anger. It is your father you need to talk with and not your mother. You need to talk with your father about those feelings and we can do it in this group." Jay seemed somewhat perplexed about Bobby's statement but felt a measure of relief (He could discuss his father, but not his mother, he thought to himself): "What exactly do you mean that we can do it here in this group?" "Jay, the "empty-chair technique" can be utilized. If you want to do the work involved, I will assist in setting up the situation including some psycho-drama dynamics and we can request additional support from your fellow group members as well. Are you willing to do that; i.e., to take the risk?" Jay thought for a minute and said, with some reservations, "If you think it will help me, I agree to try." "Fine, but first let's talk, as a group, regarding anger per se."

"Anger is a "luxury that alcoholics (or drug addicts, for that matter) can ill afford" (AA Big Book). It is much too costly, the price being too high." Jay could not contain his need to comment at this point, "What do you mean by that?" Bobby glanced over toward Jay, "Well, the alcoholic or drug addict historically doesn't handle anger very appropriately. Serenity and anger cannot co-exist within the recovering individual. Serenity encompasses sobriety and anger and serenity do not mix! Given the addict's inability to calm and soothe "self," within the anger situation, a preferred drug is utilized rather than the utilization of healthy coping mechanisms. In addition, because of 'state dependent learning', he continued, chronic use of alcohol tends to magnify (exacerbates) any problem the drinker encounters; i.e., greater levels of frustration, anxiety, failures, isolation, impatience, or perceived negative reactions to life's daily demands (anger in this instance). Anger is exaggerated or is triggered by the slightest hint of criticism, for example, by another person. The long and short of it equates to a relapse to addictive behaviors, as previously discussed; the price you will pay for out-of-control anger episodes is a return to your active addiction." Period! "Is that explanation adequate?" Jay nodded in agreement and Bobby continued. "Anger is nothing more than a feeling but when anger is a characteristic of a past event rather than a present event it becomes disruptive to your well-being and is absolutely counterproductive to your recovery efforts. Additionally, when more emotion (feelings) than appears to be warranted is involved in a present event, the odds are that some direct link with a past event has occurred; the unresolved anger of today emerging from the past. Part of the learning process in this group relates to the enhancement of your awareness that mostly it is "you" who is angry with "yourself". The comic strip character (Pogo) phrased it nicely and I paraphrase: 'We have met the enemy and he is we'.

This process is called "beating yourself up" and the addicted individual is an expert in this arena. The recovering alcoholic or drug addict in order to sustain his efforts at recovery must move toward a more realistic and fulfilling method of coping with anger and communicating anger more appropriately. This process includes becoming more sensitive to the needs and feelings of others through confronting others with care, concern, honesty, and directness; the subtle difference between 'aggressiveness and assertiveness'. Paradoxically, anger is often times an emotional response that is triggered or emerges in direct opposition to the amount of hurt that has been experienced; i.e., the more angry the group member appears, the greater the probability that he is protecting the *self* from hurts inflicted from the past, like shame, guilt, or issues of abandonment.

Jay again interrupted, "Bobby, are you saying that my anger, my anxiety, could be issues of abandonment as a child?" "Could be, Jay," Bobby responded. "Maybe it is time for the empty chair and some psycho-drama techniques. Are you ready to work?" Jay nodded hesitantly. "First, throughout the process, you will be in complete control of the drama as it unfolds here in the group. Someone in group can volunteer to role-play (not to be) your father. Do you want to pick a member to role-play your father?" Jay pointed toward

Howard and he agreed. Bobby motioned for Howard to take the chair that had been placed in front of Jay by Janice, the Co-facilitator. Howard slowly took the chair, looking directly into Jay's eyes. Bobby further explained, "Jay you will be the writer in this role-play and no one is allowed to ad-lib? Do you understand? Howard, do you understand?" Both men indicated they understood the instructions. The process unfolded slowly initially as in any dialogue between two people with the nervousness, the timidity, and the "unsureness." With each confrontation (and there were many) Jay began to soften his "attacks." It was difficult for Bobby to glean an attitudinal change or a tiredness of the process, but Jay sounded different with the spoken words directed toward the man who was "role-playing" his father. Howard appeared to be more emotionally invested in the process than Jay but both men had tears when the drama ended. Prior to Bobby speaking to formally terminate the drama, Jay hugged Howard who then returned to his chair. A silence swept over the group and before Bobby could speak Rene spoke up," Seeing you express your anger toward your father has helped me a lot. Maybe there is a chance that I can do what you have begun. I have never allowed myself to do that in the past. I keep hearing the voice inside my head that admonishes me. It says I'm awful if I resent my mother or if I feel anger toward her. I think today I am closer to being able to deal with my anger. And I really appreciated your honesty." Other members of the group joined in the conversation of "unexposed anger" and angry feelings toward others. Bobby sat back and listened intently. He thought to himself rather smugly, "I do love it when a plan comes together." Bobby knew Jay had opened the door for the potential of candid conversations with his father and that was exactly what he had hoped for as a result of the enacted drama. Jay could do it, but would he? That would remain the unknown element."

Jennifer glanced down at her watch. Bobby responded immediately, “Jennifer, there is no need to cue me. I know time is getting away from us today. Howard, please close the session for us?” After the Serenity Prayer, as always, hugs were exchanged as the group room emptied.

Jay headed back to the cottage prior to lunch to write out some of his thoughts concerning the group experience. Could he talk with his father with the same level of emotionality as he had talked with Howard? He felt better and decided the effort was worth it and he continued to write as he lit yet another cigarette. Jay lost track of time and was late for lunch. It was worth it, what was written said it all. He felt confident in his ability to courageously confront his father.

Chapter 17 – Alcoholics Anonymous

Jay was complying with his treatment plan and especially the attendance of the AA meetings. In the beginning, he thought they were dull and meant for those unfortunates who had nothing else in the world, but now his view was changing with every meeting. He was becoming more and more inquisitive regarding the phenomenon of Alcoholics Anonymous. He had meant to speak to Bobby about it, but the time never really presented itself. He would wait for the appropriate time and place. As he continued to sit in the rocking chair on the porch of his cottage, he recognized one of the men who brought his first glimpse of the AA program (He was the one who chaired the nightly AA meetings at WesterBrook). Jay got up out of the chair and headed toward him. His name was Tim and this was the time and place. "Tim," Jay yelled. "Do you have a minute?" "Sure," he replied. "What can I do for you?" "Well, can you explain some of the basics of the AA movement to me?" "Sure, let's sit down," he said.

Tim was an older gentleman who was warm and easy to talk with. He began where he needed to begin with Jay. "Man's basic instinct demands power to sustain life and to insure survival. Admission of complete defeat is never considered! However, the fact that all self-sufficiency has been depleted by a once completely innocuous substance and effectively unable to resist its alluring qualities, the alcoholic continues in his life of denial. Even though he is unable to recognize the incessant emotional demands and the depths of humiliation complete with physical exhaustion, the disease insidiously progresses to dominate life and create chaos at every turn. Only through admitted utter defeat will the alcoholic find the strength and the courage to live without the mind-numbing effects of alcohol. The philosophy of the self-help movement is rooted in the proposition of complete, absolute defeat of the aggressive, dysfunctional willfulness of the alcoholic. In the depths of complete and unrelenting desperation, the alcoholic being overpowered by depression and despair, begins to recognize that only by letting-go of his willfulness does he begin the journey back through the personal loss of power, he finds "the power" through defeat and hence, renewal.

Unless the alcoholic could recognize at a base level that without being in touch with the creator and sustainer of power, the supply would be exhausted. There is no regulator of the power, no alternator or generator to replace spent power without the help of a Power greater than the individual self. The alcoholic attempts to blast his way through life rather than working to live life. He attempts to force the world to fit neatly into his self-centered, predetermined set of expectations. An unwillingness to accept the world and life as it is and the insistence on making it conform to some expected image continues to bring chaos. The alcoholic absolutely refuses to accept life on life's terms. Lack of willpower was not the solution or the problem. It was the misuse of this power. He had tried to bombard problems of daily living with willpower instead of attempting to bring "his willpower" into agreement with life (God's intention). This was a hard statement to consider when his whole life has been a "running-away from such religiosities."

This coming to terms with his perceived and imagined immortality and invincibility drives the search for equilibrium and well-being. Instincts, specifically attuned to survival on the alcoholic's own terms, are described as "instincts run-riot," as evidenced by the unreasonable fear that basic instincts will not be satisfied. This drives the urge to be envious of others' possessions, to become angry when perceived needs and wants aren't fulfilled exactly to his specifications and satisfaction. Thus an inordinate pursuit of power and status becomes a driving force with the alcoholic, with an expectancy of absolute fulfillment with little or no effort being expended. He deserves it!

The absolute fear of not truly living terrifies the alcoholic in the throes of addiction. His basic instinct is toward survival and away from utter destruction because the alcoholic is programmed to survive, not to self-destruct. Strange though, this is the exact path followed by the alcoholic, slowly, almost imperceptively bent on self-destruction.

There is no single defined or described alcoholic personality per se but it seems that all alcoholics continue to be childish (not child-like), emotionally sensitive and immature, and grandiose in their actions and reactions. Developmental milestones in the emotional arena have been sidetracked. The system that attempts to cope with the aid of an outside chemical is restricted and narrow in its development; i.e., if a man begins alcohol use at, say fifteen years old, and he continues to drink for fifteen to twenty years, then he remains at age fifteen emotionally speaking. You've heard of those guys who have become trapped in the fifties or sixties. The ingrained mentality is still there today sitting in the parking lot with their hot-cars and drinking, trying to impress other people, for whatever reasons. Ambition and motivation has abandoned them."

He continued: "Martin Buber recognized that a person in crisis needs direction to navigate through the seas of misery, confusion, hopelessness, and despair" as encountered with the downward drift (progressive nature of the addictive process) of alcoholism. "Alcoholics Anonymous" further adds instructions with the required Steps to follow and having the unique ability of one alcoholic freely telling his story to another alcoholic. Anyone who has lived through a particularly intense and frightening experience with others can understand the bond that develops as a result of the memory of the experience and the gratitude of living through the experience, the camaraderie. This "bond" is perpetuated endlessly in AA meeting halls around the world.

Alcoholics Anonymous is a group of individuals who are recovering from a disease that drove them to the utter depths of despair and degradation to the conviction that life was in fact worth living to the fullest. This realization was the thought process that enabled Bill W to continue with his exploration of his sickness (He would later refer to it as a "devastating weakness"). June 10, 1935 marks the birth and infancy of the AA movement with Bill W and Dr. Bob at the helm. By 1939, the experiences of the fledging society had been compiled in a book finally entitled "Alcoholics Anonymous" (the big book so named because in those early days of the movement, paper was expensive and they had only a little money. However, cheap paper was available and came in big sheets and thus the book was dubbed "the big book").

Some things must be concealed at certain times, not because they are ugly or wrong, but because they are fragile and delicate. Bill W recognized early the significance of anonymity and confidentiality. The small boat of AA originally would have been swamped if these two concepts had not been stressed and reiterated in the literature and meetings. The program of Alcoholics Anonymous is a delicate little gift, given one day at time to those who want it. It is a process, albeit long-term, and at times a very difficult and frustrating process, that involves honesty (with self and others, especially "self"), open mindedness (regarding different attitudes, behaviors, and thoughts), and willingness (to take risks in stepping out of maladaptive behaviors into more adaptive ones); the H.O.W. of the Program. Like the desperation of the drowning man in the lake with a bystander watching him thrash about patiently waiting until he quits fighting, recognizing only then could he be saved without drowning the "rescuer". This also was a basic tenet of the AA philosophy; attraction rather than promotion. Others have attempted to help the alcoholic but their orientation in the process was, indeed, that the alcoholic simply lacked the will-power to put the dreaded, demon rum down and this in itself exacerbated the guilt, despair, shame and denial of the disease. It allowed the disease to continue to flourish. Few of them recognized that the pathological use of alcohol was the problem and tried to treat some underlying symptom."

"Jay, Alcoholics Anonymous has only suggestions and recommendations for you. AA will always be there for you and remember that as you continue with your treatment here at WesterBrook." Alcoholics Anonymous provides an explanation of the past in a way that provides hope for the future, allows the alcoholic to more effectively cope with guilt, anxiety, remorse, and confusion through mutual identification and support, provides specific behaviors that will change life in a desired direction (staying sober and working a 12-Step program) and it provides additional hope and inspiration that aides in combating demoralization. Tim further remarked that within the meetings various personal summations were offered that included the following: "I was not present for most of my life; the only perfect thing I did today was, I didn't take a drink or use any other drug, and, finally, now I am participating in my own life." Jay nodded in agreement.

"Jay, these folks were in your shoes at one time and now because of treatment and the fellowship of Alcoholics Anonymous, they offer an open invitation to you, if you so choose," to join them in their efforts to stay clean and sober "One day at a time".

Change is an ever-widening process of growth. AA helps in the growth. The 12-Steps speak beautifully to this concept of 'change': Steps 1-3 reflect the 'beginnings of change', Steps 4-9 reflect the 'process of change', and Steps 10-12 provides a measure for the 'ongoing change process'. Jay, AA makes the changing almost too simple and that simplicity keeps many alcoholics in their miserably, diseased condition. Herbert Spencer said it nicely: "There is principle which is a bar against all information, which is proof against all arguments and which cannot fail to keep a man in everlasting ignorance; that principle is contempt prior to investigation!" Consider strongly what I have told you Jay. "We" only want to help." With that being said, Tim wished Jay well as he continued on his journey to the Administration building. Jay felt a sense of relief that a "lay-person" knew so much about the disease that had tried to kill him. Tonight would be a restful night for him. Jay slowly made his way back to his room.

As Jay completed his shower and headed toward his bed, his mind began to wander and process. He had begun to enjoy the various videos and the didactic presentations which were scheduled on a daily basis. He particularly enjoyed the processing of the video material afterwards when straightforward "give and take" would always result in lively, and at times, very heated discussions. He did enjoy the adversarial relationship that seemed to evolve on each occasion and if it did not, he would certainly prod it along. For Jay, it didn't seem to matter which side he pursued. He had practice in that arena, sure enough! Of particular interest was his emerging awareness of and intrigue with spirituality and its various constructs. He had never considered spirituality as very important and further he knew nothing of the concept. A religiosity concept such as spirituality was meant to quell the masses and keep them within socio-legal boundaries with the great "father" always watching with a selfish interest. His previous thoughts of a "non-god" were slowly eroding and this "spiritual, Higher Power thing" was beginning to take shape for him and to be indeed meaningful to him, more so daily. He was also beginning to discern the subtle differences between religiosity and spirituality. The Step workshops introducing and explaining the 12-Steps (Alcoholics Anonymous) were very difficult concepts for Jay. He vowed, however, to learn of this “spiritual thing”. Jay recalled Bobby’s words regarding spirituality: Because all of us are different in many respects, the quest for spirituality (that is being in touch with your spirit) will be different. Some of you may find it through public service and others may find it through our vocation or avocation and still others through deep familial involvement. There are also some who reclaim it through their religious faith. However it is claimed or reclaimed, it is “essential” to our well-being.” It helped somewhat but he felt a strange “yearning”, a wanting to know more.

Jay began to see that he was no longer fighting himself or anybody else in his life. The past two and a half weeks had been difficult for him but with a growing hunger for this new way of life, his sense of urgency to progress internally motivated him and kept him narrowly focused.

Jay continued to measure his anxiety levels that had begun to lessen in the past five days. His individual sessions with Bobby were more open, spontaneously alive, and, definitely, more on an intimate level. He had begun to trust Bobby’s abilities and his spoken care and concern. Guilt continued to plague him and Bobby assured him that these intense feelings would remit in time and Jay made the decision to again continue to trust Bobby’s judgment. He offered little resistance now to Bobby’s suggestions and recommendations and he did not attack or play the devil’s advocate with Bobby as he had done earlier. He was no longer in the compliance mode of coping; he was learning to grow from within!

The one part of his treatment experience that really bothered him was the upcoming “family week” activities. How would

Kayce react to all of this? She had always thought Jay lacked the willpower and internal motivation, maybe maturity, to endure abstinence from alcohol. She didn't buy this "disease thing." Families devastated by internal and external violence and torn by dramatic conflicts was the image of the familial unit portrayed by the insidious disease of alcoholism. Jay knew full well what that felt like and even to think of his past deeds caused him great pain inside. Little did Jay realize that Kayce had been faithfully and regularly attending Alanon meetings and getting a real education regarding that disease thing of alcoholism. She was growing also in this spiritual thing that was beginning to fully engulf Jay's thinking. Jay was worried and anxious and his sleep disturbances were getting more intense as the fateful week approached. Thus far he had said nothing to his fellow group members or to Bobby.

Chapter 18 - Spirituality

Jay wanted very much to talk with the chaplain especially after the lecture on the "Spiritual Aspects of Recovery" but he got away before Jay could approach him. Jay decided to ask Bobby to make an appointment for him. As Jay was leaving the lecture room, he saw Bobby just walking into his office. Jay followed him inside and Bobby turned around looking somewhat surprised.

"What can I do for you?" he inquired. "Can you arrange an appointment for me to see the Chaplain?" "Yes, Jay, sit down," he said, as he picked up the telephone and made the appointment. "4:00 P.M. this afternoon OK with you?" "Sure," Jay replied. "Anything else then," Bobby inquired. "That will do it, thanks Bobby," and Jay left.

Jay was looking forward to the meeting. Jay left Bobby's office and headed for his favorite spot until his appointment at 4:00 P.M.; the rocking chair on the front porch of his cottage. Jay made a decision then and there to purchase one of these relaxing "things" when he returned home. He sat rocking away as several other group members arrived. This was considered "personal time" for them. They could wash clothes, write letters, complete task assignments, read, or just "lazy away" as Jay was taking this opportunity to do. His schedule was filled with the "rocking chair" until 4:00 P.M.

The time was now 3:30 and he decided to leave early for the Chaplain's office. He had heard many things about Karl Goshin; a short, graying, rotund man who had retired from three church assignments and who had over fifteen years of sobriety. He was an easily approachable man when he could be "corralled". He arrived and smoked a cigarette while waiting for Karl. A car drove up and there was no mistaking the identity. Karl had a "presence" even before he got out of the car. Jay walked toward him with his hand extended.

Karl hugged him and said, "Hello, Jay." This "hugging thing" was new to Jay but he, frankly speaking, enjoyed it. Together they walked into Karl's office and Jay thought to himself there's no anxiety! Karl indicated to Jay to take a seat. It was, indeed easy, no comfortable, to be around this man. No pretense, no labor, no trying to please, this man was there for all to see. After some small talk (very little of that) Karl asked, "What can I do for you, young man?"

"Well," Jay responded, "tell me more about this spiritual thing." Now Karl was able to size up a man pretty quickly and Jay seemed very earnest in his request, so Karl was glad to share with Jay and, indeed, he felt honored. That's also the feeling Jay felt. Karl got up from his chair, went over to his bookcase, and retrieved a worn copy of the "Big Book" from the shelf. "This, my boy, tells much of what you are seeking. Even your journey to my office could be called a "spiritual journey," of sorts. Spirituality is! This concept is difficult, at best, to define. Spirituality may be defined as each person reflects upon it; i.e., the breath of life that each of us possesses at birth, the essence of being, the light or spark of the divine that burns within to illuminate the journey of life and bonds us to the rest of creation and humanity. As troubles of life began to be overpowering and coupled this with a concomitant pre-disposition toward addictive behaviors, the light (the spirit; the "awareness" of the light) begins to glow dimmer until only a flicker of what "was" remains. With the dimming of the spirit a loss of power is felt and a concomitant feeling of an absence. Additionally, as the glow becomes dimmer, to a flicker, we become depressed, angry, confused, despondent, apathetic, and/or a combination of all of these negative states.

Some automatically equate spirituality to religiosity. Spirituality is a "one-to-one" relationship whereas religiosity deals with a vast body of knowledge and in a mass group process. This is not to say that spirituality does not exist in religiosity. It can and does exist alongside the religions of the world. It also embraces faith, good will, and love of fellow man. The journey to deep religious conviction, in my opinion, can and does begin with a "spiritual stirring" or in the common vernacular of the 12-Step movement, "a spiritual awakening." The awakening has two components. One is a pervasive sense of an "absence" (described as a thought from deep within) and a slowly building awareness of a presence (a happening "to us"). An event occurs that intervenes to shake the individual out of his usual patterns of thoughts and response behaviors into a very different view of the world and his place within it. The "wonder" response is activated or maybe reactivated by this profound change that has occurred. "Softness" has replaced the "hardness of the heart." That impregnable fortress, built by the person to keep society out and the self imprisoned, has crumbled. Child-like curiosity and wonder return with the ability to be astonished! To be incapable of "surprise" is to be less than a fully functioning person. This gift is reclaimed in the process of spiritual attainment. In this process of becoming a spiritual person you will embark on a very personal and intimate educational journey. You begin to reclaim your child-like belief in fairies, fairy dust, the Easter Bunny, and Santa Claus. The recovery or the re-discovery of the honesty of a child in relating to others and to the world can be profound and the notion of an ultimate companionship enters the heart to the very soul of existence.

Spirituality is much more about "humanness" than about "Godliness." It's about getting involved with another with developing the ability to get outside one's own immediate concerns to perform a selfless act for another. It is concerned with the ability through changed attitudes and behaviors, to relate to others, to ourselves, and to a Power Greater than self. Spirituality is simply a chosen positive way of living considering self, others and society in general. Four movements mark the journey in spiritual attainment: From fear to trust, from self-pity to gratitude, from resentment to acceptance, and from dishonesty to honesty. Spiritual attainment is growth and movement away from self-centeredness. In essence, it is a blending of the courageousness of the young with the courtesy of the more mature through commitment and action, submission, and the recognition and presence of vulnerability. Acquired knowledge and reclaimed "wonder" combine to re-ignite the spirit to a brilliance long forgotten. The life of spirituality is central and essential to the program of recovery upon which you will embark."

Karl purposely waxed philosophically throughout the discourse he provided to Jay. Karl was a "counselor of people" and he knew of Jay's soft heart. He had attended to Jay's right-brain and left the analytical and intellectual stuff to the left-brain to wrestle out. Jay thanked Karl for his time and his sensitivity in presenting this information to him. From the expression on Jay's face, Karl went one step further. Karl smiled sympathetically and spoke in his most self-mocking tone: "I used to think, what are my sufferings compared to what Our Lord went through? But then it occurred to me, except for the last three days, he had a pretty good time." Both laughed heartily and Jay readily grasped what Karl had tried to present to him. Another "gift!"

Karl had one final thought to leave with Jay. He continued, "This journey you will embark upon toward self-truth (the spiritual meaning of life for you) is a worthy pursuit but the final destination could be dangerous to the psyche, especially what is encountered on the journey of self-discovery via the search for "truth." Uncertainty as a constant companion but motivated by the desire to find the promises of sobriety, the recovering alcoholic continues despite the roadblocks that life sets in his path. Uncertainty does not always imply a negative stance but can be seen as a part of the process of growth. Uncertainty can lead quite readily to tolerance (could he be right?), tolerance can lead to a multiplicity in viewpoints and theory, and this divulgence can lead to an appreciation of the complexity, ambiguity, and the transience nature that all characterize "reality" and change. Useful illusions, vital lies, and exotic beliefs provide the hope and promise that an answer does, in fact, exist. Treatment provides the framework and the nourishing environment where the search can be safely initiated. Some of these beliefs are seen on clubhouse (AA meetings) walls around the world; i.e., "Easy does it," "One day at a time," "This too, shall pass," "Progress, not perfection," and "Let it happen!" to name just a few."

"Jay, a person needs two anchors in life to weather the storms. One is a collection of good friends. Not a gathering of acquaintances or drinking buddies but friends who love you, "warts and all." Friends I call "midnight friends." Friends who are there for you during your darkest hours are indispensable to life lived well. The second anchor is a burning, passionate cause. It amazes me the number of people who waste so much time and energy on second-class causes. Don't waste your time on a cause that does not fire your imagination and initiative. The main reason people are so tired today is because they wear themselves out running from cause to cause. Find your special cause and devote your time and energy to it. Be sure it is worthwhile and will make a lasting contribution to those who come after you. When you find your "cause" and dedicate yourself to it alone, you will find you no longer go to bed fatigued nor do you awaken tired. You will be full of energy and vitality, looking forward to each new day!"

It was now 5:30 P.M. and almost time for dinner. Karl got up and walked toward Jay. Jay knew the session was at an end but wished for more. Jay was first to extend "the hug" and Karl seemed to be pleased. It felt as if Jay had always known this man. Karl handed Jay a piece of paper as they walked outside and Jay continued to the cafeteria.

Walking toward the cafeteria, Jay unfolded the paper and read the words printed on the page:

"Where did I leave it? Surely I didn't lose it! I had it just the other day. It was so lovely, bright and sparkly. No! It isn't gone, just mislaid. I'll find it when I'm not really looking, there it will be! I'll find it, Surely I will.
Not here, not there, not anywhere! How could it have slipped away without my knowing? Such a loss couldn't go unnoticed. And when, oh, when did I lose it? Last week? Last year? When?
Ah, there it is! My granddaughter has it! See it sparkle and how lovely! Why, she doesn't even know she has it!
Of course, neither did I, not until it was gone. I didn't lose it!
I gave it to her. And, she'll look for it one day only to realize that she has given it to her grandchild.
Such a gift; lovely, bright and sparkly,
And temporary."

(Liz Cauthorn, 1993)

Jay's eyes could not contain the tears and, indeed, he had been given a cherished "gift" by Karl who was smiling and waving goodbye to him. This was the experience he had hoped to have.

Chapter 19 - Introspection

As simple as the solution appeared to others, Jay worked against the truth as hard as any man would defend his home and family from invaders. For him, life and his reactions to it were not to be contradicted and pushed aside as worthless. He had accomplished much in his short life and now simply because he had developed the disease of alcoholism, all of it was said to be a "sham." This he could not tolerate! Jay was again missing the point of the conversation; when his life was at stake his "clarity of thought" escaped him and left him with very primitive defenses and the negative coping skills of projection (blaming), rationalizing (making excuses), and intellectualizations (looking at behaviors rather than the associated feelings or talking about the feelings without any corresponding affect). When he felt under attack he resorted to "fight or flight" and mostly it was "flight!" His ordinarily exceptional coping skills eluded his grasp!

With each confrontation he felt less of a man; his massive facade of defensiveness was crumbling and with each breach came the potential for renewed life. Bobby continued to listen to Jay as he groped in the darkness of despair of his alcoholism. Jay was allowed to continue to feel the paradoxical nature of his disease; the double edged sword that existed to kill him, spiritually, if not physically. Jay was indeed struggling with Step One and Bobby could not lessen the pain for him. The crisis that brought Jay to this place and time must be examined again and again to illuminate the full impact of his life's unmanageability and powerlessness. Bobby could not separate the good or not-so-good aspects for Jay; that was Jay's job to accomplish. That task remains the essence of Jay's treatment. Jay's counselor was aware that he was afraid to explore further and maybe this was enough for this session. Bobby offered Jay a "time-out" for now, to allow Jay the time he needed and "deserved." Bobby suggested that Jay walk down to the stream, sit down, and watch as the water came to him, stayed with him, and continued onward downstream; observe the effortlessness manner in which nature creates and formulates the needed acceptance required of Step One. Jay agreed to the break and left Bobby seated. Bobby moved toward his bay-window watching Jay walk toward the stream.

As Jay stood by the rippling waters of the brook that coursed its way past his assigned cottage, he began to regress to simpler times in his life.

Jay's subconscious made a decision for him and his early days prior to the difficulties of adult-hood came clearly to him. Jay's early school years were mostly uneventful until the fifth grade when he became involved with little league baseball. This sport became an all-consuming obsession and dominated his every thought and behavior. Baseball equipment and various pennants decorated every square inch of his bedroom. He played third base on the White Sox team until the coach recognized that he had an "arm" and moved him to the pitcher's mound. Jay enjoyed the control this position provided to him. He won many games and he further thought the winnings were of his own making because he did pitch and did strike out many batters. This pattern of winning would be his undoing in the future but he knew nothing about losing; only winning! During the school term, his obsession with this game caused conflicts at home. He absolutely would lose himself in a televised baseball game forgetting the time and the getting up in the morning for school. It required much effort for his Mother to finally arouse him out of bed for breakfast and then off to school on time. Actually it became an ordeal for both of them. His father was always out of the house by 7:00 A.M. so this morning ritual was consigned on a regular basis to his mother. Finally in a last desperate attempt to resolve this issue once and for all, his mother issued the "mother of all ultimatums": Either get up on your own on a school morning or the television would be turned off at 9:00 P.M. This came as a big surprise to Jay. He had not been held accountable before, so why this "ultimatum" now? This was but the beginning of the conflict that was growing, albeit secretively, between himself and his parents, particularly his father. Where was he when Jay needed his support and encouragement? After all, wasn't baseball the all American past-time? And why shouldn't Jay indulge? It wasn't as if this went on twelve months out of the year. Jay had needed his father to be present at those games and especially at the Championship game. (A father's approval and votes of confidence are necessary ingredients for the beginnings of "self-confidence" of youth that leads to a more mature confidence in later years.) After a long season of thirty-six little league games, Jay's team (the White Sox) had won the Championship of Class Double A. Jay then was able to again settle back into his normal routine with school. Even after the last game of the season, he was becoming preoccupied with the next year's season. He had taped many of the games on the VCR and some would be played over and over again. His schooling didn't suffer because he had the ability to be strictly task-oriented when it was absolutely necessary. And school did not demand much of his intellectual powers anyway. He seemed to always come out on top; much like the cat that falls and recovers each time upright and appearing no worse off for the experience. However, the seventh grade pony-league team brought a severe disappointment to him. To his utter amazement he could not hit a "curve ball." His mother took him to the eye doctor and glasses were prescribed for him. This didn't help the situation at all. Now the ball, as it was hurled toward him, was very visible to the extent that he could see the individual stitches on the ball but still he could not hit a damn "curve ball." After several agonizing attempts (four games), he resigned from the team (told his coach and other players that he was tired of all the hassles of the game and told his parents that the sport was now demanding too much of his school time. He stored his equipment neatly in the attic and spoke nothing more about it.

A jet blasted the silence and Jay was again with his disturbing thoughts. His daydream revealed much and he, felt, for the first time, that maybe this program could work for him. Always winning and feeling on top of the world as defined by his experience may have been faulty, at best, but he was willing to take that risk now. His past had, in fact, come to him, stayed, and continued downstream. The good and not-so-good times experienced when using alcohol merged at times but he knew about his "selective memory functioning" from one of the lectures presented by the Medical Director and he was fully aware of the inherent danger. From Bobby he had learned earlier to dispute the over-riding good times and always be cognizant of the certain fact that he was "alcoholic." And if he ever forgot that very important fact, he was in big trouble! Step one was the Step that he would rely heavily upon especially in his early recovery efforts. Life's unmanageability and his powerlessness as a result of alcohol use were facts that he could not afford to forget. It was easy for most to give "lip-service" to this Step. The concept of "acceptance" and not simple compliance permeated the very fabric of the Step and Jay knew it must be generalized to the outside world if his life was to change. He had been reading many articles including those written by William James and Eric Fromm. James remarked that "most of us live in a very restricted circle of potential being; that we further ignore our strengths and (routinely) follow our (inherent) weaknesses"; Fromm stated that "living is the process of continuous rebirth; the tragedy is that we die before we are fully born!" These statements had stuck in Jay's consciousness and they aptly described his life of alcohol. His inappropriate, pathological use of alcohol effectively robbed him of being truly alive, numbed his feelings and exacerbated and magnified negative situations and feelings. The substance that had given him so much pleasure and satisfaction in the past was now trying to kill him. He knew that without any reservations!

Chapter 20 – Termination of Treatment

The other group members continued for some time to listen to the various reasons given by Shane for leaving treatment prematurely. Shane reasoned that others didn't trust him and made fun of him behind his back. When queried about his apparent lack of trust for the group or the process and his profound secretiveness, he retaliated with more shows of anger and hostility. Each in turn tried to persuade Shane to stay and finish what he and the group had started. Jennifer related her early group difficulties and how she had felt initially especially about the trust issue and her feelings of paranoia. Jay responded with a resounding, "Yes." Rene by now was bored with the process and told him to leave if that's what he really wanted to do! Rene, without knowing it, had struck a nerve and Shane's facial expression softened. Bobby said almost in a whisper to Shane, "What do you want from us?" Shane didn't reply. Bobby again posed the question to the group. "If this was happening to the group as a whole, what might the group want?" Bobby had hoped that by reframing his request to a "what if" philosophical request, the anxiety of responding would become less. Many answers were given by various group members; i.e. attention, support from the group, understanding without question, protection from verbal assaults, closeness, etc.

Everyone else but Shane had a response. He continued to sit and stare at the floor. He was picking at his fingers and tapping his right foot exhibiting a high level of anxiety. Bobby spoke directly to Shane.

"Shane, I understand that you are anxious and perhaps feeling very much alone right now. But I want you to know that I am very concerned about your wanting to leave treatment". Shane's facial expression again seemed to relax but with a renewed intenseness in his eyes. He knew Bobby was being up-front with him but he could not bring himself to accept Bobby's concern. His anger returned quickly and this time he directed his assault toward Bobby.

"You don't really give a shit about whether I stay or whether I go! You have your family, your job, your "things," yourself! I've lost everything to cocaine and I've decided there's no reason for me to stay here any longer! I'm going and that is that." Shane then got up from his chair as if to leave. The other group members had a look of disbelief on their faces. Their collective thoughts involved how would the counselor now handle this situation?

Bobby sat still with direct eye contact with Shane. Shane was poised for a fight if the situation escalated to it. Bobby was quick to recognize the growing anger and could see the rage behind the eyes of a frightened and emotionally wounded man.

Remaining in his chair and looking up toward Shane he began, "Shane, your decision seems to be set and your voice seems pretty adamant about leaving here. Your anger and anxiety tells me more is going on with you than meets the eye. You've been in this group for three weeks and I believe strongly that your fellow group members respect you and care for you. Up to this point, you have been compliant and cooperative. I do care about whether you go or whether you stay." (At this point, Shane tried to interrupt but Bobby tactfully pointed out, that at least now, he could listen to him, because he had sat quietly and listened for the past half hour to him.) Shane accepted that and remained quiet while Bobby continued: "You have made some real progress and for you, a need does exist deep within you to complete this thing you've started. Allow yourself that privilege and consider the letter you wrote to Cocaine and the way you described how cunning and powerful the Lady really was and how she could tease you back to her. Bobby had to stress the hopeless nature of the disease of addiction and asked Shane to consider again the crisis that prompted him to enter treatment. "Shane, I will neither abandon nor will I sit in judgment of you because you chose to express a feeling in this group. You know how your fellow group members feel about you. I think they, too, will stay with you as you grow. Remember also, that your best decision making processes in the past resulted in all the losses you've mentioned and was the motivating force behind you being admitted to WesterBrook." Bobby had handled the attack by Shane in a non-defensive and non-retaliatory fashion. He knew that any group that was able to tolerate negative feelings directed toward the counselor by a group member (as Shane had just done) would be invariably strengthened by the experience. That act would function as a catalyst in bringing the group closer. Additionally, the group gains a deeper level of trust toward the process and the counselor.

Shane slowly sat back down as tears began to slowly roll down his cheeks. "I expected you to attack me for being angry with you," he said through his tears. "You are right. I do need to complete this. I'm sorry I said those things to you and to the group. Can you forgive me?"

Bobby replied with warmness, "Shane, can you forgive yourself?" By this time his tears were flowing. He couldn't respond. He was now defeated. Bobby allowed him to experience the emotional cleansing in full. Finally he said to the group, "To each of you, my friends, I am sorry. I'd like to continue with my treatment. Life for me in the past has been centered on romancing my drug use but today my focus needs to be on my romancing recovery instead of the drug."

After comments from the other group members, Bobby spoke, "I am proud of the courage you displayed in making your new commitment to recovery. Today is a milestone for you. You have been mostly hidden, but today you are visible and you are real. Thank you for allowing us to see the whole person today."

"Let's close now with the Serenity Prayer and hugs," Bobby said. When the prayer was completed, hugs were exchanged all around. Slowly the group room emptied of the participants involved in the magic of today.

Alone, Bobby sat down and again repeated the Serenity Prayer being thankful for the wonderfully alive group experience that had just occurred. Awe, astonishment, and "fairy dust" still exist in the miracle of change and thus the spiritual aspects of the process were very clear to Bobby as he considered the events of the past ninety minutes.

Chapter 21 - The Relapse

"To comfort the disturbed and to disturb the comfortable is not intended to disturb those who are comfortable in a healthy sobriety, but it is intended to disturb the naively comfortable" (Staying Sober, Gorski/Miller, 1986). This was a strong statement by Bobby to utter as he continued to explain various aspects of relapse to Jay. Relapse scared Jay and he wanted more than the lecture provided by Jeremy Daniels, the Program Director. His treatment plan was progressing satisfactorily; at least that was what he was told by Bobby via the Clinical Staffings held weekly. Jay was able to recognize some growth and a definite change in his attitudes. Jay recognized now for the first time, that striving for perfection was an absolute waste of his time and effort. He was becoming "mellow" about just being human and wondrously alive. He especially liked the affirmation he was given during a lecture on "Positive Thinking to Growth": "I will live today as best I can and tomorrow I will do even better." Jay was indeed learning to plan for future events but he was not getting trapped into "planning the results" again. He liked that. "No longer must I be driven by my compulsive need to please other people, he said to himself." "Freedom is great!" he pondered. But he made the decision to seek Bobby's input into the other part of the equation and that being the obsession that is normally connected to the compulsiveness to act. He had heard that if the thought to return to chemical use did not cause a relapse, then the compulsiveness would virtually guarantee a relapse: Both of these masters of human behaviors, obsessions and compulsions, would require intensive attention because if they are left unchecked, another guarantee of relapse: A return to the life of drinking that had threatened to kill him in the past. Previous thoughts of sitting in his garage with the pistol cocked, reared righteously in the depths of his soul and that scared Jay and within his mind, he had to master the monster or it would surely master his life as it had done in the past. He would not forget.

Bobby was continuing and Jay's full attention was now again focused on his words. "Relapse is a progressive return to a symptomatic pattern of alcohol use. Jay, there is more to relapse than this cut and dry statement. The relapse syndrome indicates a failure to develop effective alternatives for dealing with day to day life stresses in a constructive, positive manner. The only correct answer to the question of why did I get drunk? Is this: I failed to do everything necessary to remain sober! An alcoholic or drug addict may relapse through neglect of responsible living patterns rather than through conscious preparation. It's what he doesn't do that induces and triggers the relapse process." "That's a rather simple way to put it," Jay commented. "Yes, Bobby responded, and Dr. Bob (AA) said in his last talk that perhaps relapse would not be done with malice aforethought, but relapse would be done as a result of extreme carelessness and indifference. The guilt that emerges with the use of alcohol after a period of abstinence re-activates the disease of alcoholism and this guilt may fuel further episodes of use. It might even be considered a guarantee to a full-blown relapse episode of use because the guilt that surfaces may be all consuming. The individual may not be able to find his way back to recovery and abstinence when this extended period occurs. His ego might prevent him from asking for help or seeking help and death may occur."

Bobby continued: "The response to the relapse is the crucial matter because the event is not to be judged or described as a failure but as a further opportunity to gain an increased awareness of the disease that has truly engulfed the alcoholic's life. Warning signs are always present but the alcoholic may not be able to recognize them as such. And, to a certain degree, he or she may not want to recognize them.

Jay, you should become aware of and familiar with your own personal relapse warning signs with the use of the "H.A.L.T." concept; for an example: Don't get too hungry, angry, lonely, or tired. Perhaps another can be added: Don't get too timid! At times being very assertive is quite necessary as you navigate through the seas (both calm and at times, rather stormy) of sobriety. Any two of these in combination can be deadly to your recovering status." This bit of information startled Jay and he was trying to understand as Bobby continued. "Bewilderments, fears, and resentments can creep back into your life. Personal suffering emerges as the result of inner pain because performances and accomplishments in recovery have not lived up to those unrealistic expectations and extremely strong perfectionistic standards that the alcoholic possesses."

Jay felt an urge to interrupt with a question. It was not really a question but more like a comment: "Bobby, I am perfectionistic and I've been working on that difficulty. I know it's a waste of time to strive for perfection but for me today it's acceptable to strive for progress. In the past it's been just as you have described it; my unrealistic expectations and perfectionism nearly killed me, but no more!" "Jay, there's more to this thing than making verbal commitments. Great discomfort can be generated that could make a return to drinking, not only possible, but desirable. (Jay's hearing became very sensitive as this subject might be the question and the answer he wanted to ask of Bobby earlier). Symptoms of relapse include apprehension about well-being, blatant denial, adamant commitment to sobriety (the alcoholic convinces himself that he will never drink again and the urgency in pursuing a daily program of recovery diminishing rather rapidly with no further motivation to continue), and unrecognized stressful situations. These and other symptoms create the fertile ground for the return to out of control use of alcohol or other drugs.

Many are in an emotional or mental relapse prior to the physical relapse. This can be described as the "dry-drunk syndrome" portrayed by the 12-Step Program of Alcoholics Anonymous. "Dry" refers to the fact that one abstains from drinking and "drunk" signifies a deeply pathological condition resulting from the use of alcohol (use of alcohol in the past). These words suggest "intoxication without alcohol!" Since intoxication is derived from a Greek word meaning "poison," a "dry-drunk" implies a state of mind and a mode of behavior that are poisonous to the alcoholic's well-being. Those experiencing a "dry-drunk" are removed from the world of sobriety because they fail to accept the necessary conditions for sober living. Their mental and emotional homes are chaotic, their approach to everyday living is unrealistic, and their behavior, both verbally and physically is unacceptable." "I understand. My life would be just as chaotic and in as much turmoil even though I'm not drinking," Jay interjected (Jay, at this point realized, that, indeed, his previous question and concern had been answered rather nicely.). Bobby indicated agreement with Jay's remark and continued, "A relapse can be a learning experience if the consequences are not severe, as in death or commitment to an institution for the rest of your life. A re-commitment to sobriety is necessary at this point. Further, relapse may evidence the need for personal adjustment in living arrangements, changing playmates and playgrounds, and/or resolving family conflicts or vocational concerns. These areas of the disease may have been overlooked or trivialized while in primary treatment. This is the specific reason for you to be honest and open-minded, especially in the group process. The alcoholic must begin to accept and work through the state of life his pathological use of alcohol has created for him and find his niche in sobriety. Relapse may often be a means to escape the life drinking has, in fact, created. Attending Continuing Care sessions, regular attendance of 12-Step meetings and getting a sponsor and utilizing that sponsor can aid the relapse prone individual to recognize that change takes time. You didn't get sick overnight and you're not going to get well overnight. To further recognize and internalize that the only permanence in life is, in fact, change. And Jay, for you, this is one of those lessons to swallow and digest that we discussed earlier.

"Concomitantly, these relapse prone individuals may have other mental or emotional problems that must be dealt with in a caring and sensitive manner. The alcoholic as a result of his long-standing "self-centeredness" needs an intellectual (mental cognition) and emotional acceptance and concomitant awareness of his disease without reservations or bitterness. He must internalize a need to accept others and, their needs, with a respect for others and their needs. If a person recovers physically (abstains from alcohol or other drugs) but fails to recover mentally, spiritually, and emotionally, his illness continues to limit him. Abstinence alone is only partial recovery."

"Treatment, then, is just the beginning," Jay said. Bobby agreed with Jay and continued, "Yes, the individual must make a commitment to become involved in a daily structured program for ongoing recovery and sobriety that will challenge him to re-learn thought patterns, emotional habits, and behavioral patterns that have been crippled in the course of his developing disease. Recovery from alcoholism or other drug addiction is much like walking up a down escalator. There is no such thing as "standing still!" When the recovering person attempts to stand still he finds himself moving backwards. Both recovery and relapse are ongoing processes rather than an "event." The alcoholic or drug addict is either in the process of recovering or he is in the process of relapse." "Another precise description, Bobby," Jay was pleased to state. He was absorbing!

"Some studies show up to 80% of those leaving a treatment center relapse and .AA has shown 68% (exact figures are not known). There are an estimated 25,000,000 alcoholics and drug addicts and roughly 15% of these get some type of treatment other than AA affiliation. Statistics further reveal that 1 of 16 maintains sobriety for any length of time (two years of more). Are you beginning to get a grasp of this cunning, baffling and powerful disease? Until the alcoholic or drug addict accepts the "dire need" to permanently abstain from alcohol or other addictive substances and participates actively in a program destined and designed to change his way of life, his efforts at recovery will most likely end in relapse. It is tantamount to your recovery that you begin to recognize the deadly aspects of relapse and of your disease of addiction.

The self-help programs reiterate that dealing with sobriety is a daily grind at times. Initially it seems too foreign to suit his tastes because the addicted person is not accustomed to the negatives he may be experiencing. Learning through practicing the 12-Steps, learning the difference between wants (which are never satisfied) and needs (which are always provided for), and learning to reject fantasizing and accepting the reality of this disease and life's difficulties, will aid you in your search for solid recovery and quality sobriety."

"Thanks for taking this time with me today. I can say I want my life to be different. In the past, I thought I knew everything but the longer I remain here, the more I learn of life in general and of myself." Bobby walked Jay to the door and watched him as he walked toward the cottage.

Bobby's thoughts of Jay's seriousness about this program intruded once again but Bobby quickly dismissed the intrusive thought and recognized that today; he could sit back and watch Jay grow in his own way and at his own speed. He did not have to push or pull. Today he was walking along side of Jay just as he had promised to do in the very beginning.

Bobby had requested Jay to meet him at his office immediately after the group session tomorrow morning to discuss discharge planning.

Jay took a very naive view of the reasons behind the appointment. What does it take to be discharged from here, he pondered. His thoughts returned to the mountains of paperwork and documents he had signed upon being admitted and he decided well, maybe it is a big deal. On a lighter side, he recalled one of the documents that he had signed that relieved WesterBrook from any responsibility for negative outcomes of treatment. At the time he signed it he was antagonist toward the clerk but signed it anyway. What an egotistical, self-centered, bastard I was then, Jay mused. Of course today, he understood the logic behind the document: He could be shown the road to recovery but no one could force him to take it.

Tonight was another AA meeting night and after that Jay vowed to turn in early. This had been an emotionally tiring day for him and he looked forward to a restful and peaceful night of sleep. His thoughts faded to his love for Kayce as he drifted off to sleep.

Chapter 22 - Bringing Closure

The weather was nice he thought as the cool morning air blew gently across the open patio. It seemed to bring a refreshing spirit to his early morning "arisings." Previous to his admission, getting up to "smell the roses" was unheard of in his life. But for the past two weeks this had indeed become a ritual for him. It was quiet and he surely did enjoy it. In an existential way, his life was changing and he considered and drew a nice parallel between his newly acquired love for the "mornings" and the "new born baby." His life was, indeed, beginning anew. A thought flashed about that terrible accident and the near death of that young woman. That event, not withstanding its seriousness, had given birth to this awakening in body and spirit. Jay accepted this in a grateful way, refusing to get "sucked into those negatives" and continued with his good thoughts. This was another example of "powerlessness" and he couldn't change the past. He, too, had experienced the pain of the accident, not physically, but mentally and emotionally which bore heavily upon him at times.

The sun was just coming up over the horizon and with it came strains of golden essence. A warm bath was the thought that occurred to him as he sat there soaking in the rays. As he sat there looking back over the past three weeks, he felt he had accomplished much. He now knew of his disease of alcoholism and that he wasn't such a "bad" guy after all. "Spirituality" (a new concept for him) had entered his life (a fledging experience but he would help it grow). He wanted recovery and he now had a fairly good grasp of the relapse process of his disease. With all of the above, he wondered what else Bobby would have for him during "that discharge session" scheduled later today.

Other residents of the cottage began to stir about. Nathan walked out onto the patio, stretching and yawning and sat down next to Jay. "Morning," Nathan grumbled. Jay replied, "Did you have another restless night? Your voice sounds like it." Nathan was slow to respond and he did have a restless night. He was concerned about the family week deal but he chose not to disclose the "concern" to Jay. He chose the easy way out and just said, "About like yours, I guess." Someone had made more coffee and Jay offered to bring Nathan a cup. He declined the offer and managed to say, "No thanks." Jay slowly got up from his rocker and left Nathan alone on the patio. When he returned with his coffee, Nathan was leaning against one of the patio posts. "What's bothering you this morning?" Nathan glanced at Jay and gave no verbal response. The non-verbal response included shrugging his shoulders and turning away. Jay knew intuitively that something was bothering Nathan but he didn't want to talk now. Jay would honor that request. Jay remembered what Bobby had said in group that first day regarding "confrontation": "You are most useful as a "confronter" of behaviors and attitudes when you are not so much attempting to change another person as when you are trying to help him or her begin to see "the self" more accurately." Bobby had further said that if one person could not see himself in others, he was in "big trouble." Jay could see himself clearly in Nathan's overall manner and he wanted to tell him so but he thought it would be more appropriate to confront Nathan in the group session this morning. By now all the cottage residents were up and getting prepared for breakfast and the beginnings of a new day. Howard was talkative this morning but found it slow going with Nathan. Jay also noticed that Howard had tried to push Nathan to discuss what was bothering him and he got a rather cold response. The cafeteria was open now for breakfast and the group left to get in line. Jay continued to be preoccupied with the session with Bobby but in a way, he was looking forward to it.

Group began as scheduled with the opening of the Serenity Prayer and some administrative remarks by Bobby and Janice. Bobby then moved right into the process. He asked if anyone had some unfinished business from yesterday's group. No one said anything. Today the group was rather quiet. Bobby sat motionless and said nothing. Jay wanted very much to say something to Nathan but he held back just long enough for Howard to speak first. Nathan was not forthcoming with the issue to be shared in group regarding his down attitude, so Howard finally began. "Bobby, I have something today. It's not mine but I feel like it could be. Nathan, Why are you so down today? This morning you were rude to everyone. I care about every person in this group. They have shown me love, support, encouragement, and caring. I want to personally extend these same "gifts" to you. How can we help you today? You seem to be hurting and when you hurt, I hurt too." The group was quiet with all eyes directed toward Nathan. They were expecting a response. Nathan felt the pressure exerted upon him by the question. It seemed as if each set of eyes were riveted right onto him. Nathan sat upright from his slouched position and turned to face Howard. Nathan sat and glared at Howard as if he was carefully measuring him for a direct frontal assault. That didn't happen.

An expression of pain spread across Nathan's face and Bobby knew the situation was well under control. "I know I was rude this morning. I also know that I can count on this group to help me. I doubted that once but not today. Howard, thank you, for your concern and I know it took courage for you to speak up like this. The short of the story is simply that I'm afraid I'm going to lose my family to this damn disease I have! This upcoming family week scares the crap out of this two-hundred, ninety pound man. Today I can say that out loud; before I could not have revealed that some person, place, thing, or situation scared me. Well, today I've said it and all of the above does scare me. I have been so preoccupied and self-centered that I forgot about this group as a valuable resource of support and caring in times of crisis. I will not forget that in the future. I still feel fearful and I appreciate the "care-frontation" Howard. You're a good man."

The pain slowly dissipated from Nathan's face and was replaced by a calmness that spread rapidly and dramatically. Howard got up from his chair and met Nathan in the middle of the group room and exchanged hugs. Bobby commented on the improved "togetherness" (cohesiveness) of the group and the way it exhibited its caring and encouraging attitude. "Howard, the term you used, "care-frontation," that's an elegant way of defining the whole process and I like it." At this point Jay spoke, "Nathan, thank you for finally giving me the courage to speak up about my fear of family week. This family week business has already occupied too much of my time and energy. I have tried to deny my anxiety about it. I tried not to think about it. Do you recognize the "I" in all this? My addiction has taught me well. I can't resolve it but I believe "we" can talk about it. The power in this group is strong and the process continues to amaze me. With your help, I know that I can do what is necessary. Facing that fear of losing my family hurts deeply but today I can be responsible for my behaviors."

Bobby thanked everyone for sharing and reinforced the group process as an interpersonal arena for the resolution of interpersonal difficulties. The Serenity Prayer was said and hugs were exchanged as if everyone knew the power that had been displayed in the session. As they filed from the room, Bobby reminded Jay of the appointment. Jay replied that he would be at his office at 11:00 A.M. Bobby indicated to Jay that would be fine.

As Bobby watched Jay walk away, he thought of the courage that was exhibited during the session by Nathan, Jay, and Howard.

Jay headed for the break area for a cup of coffee and a cigarette prior to meeting with Bobby. He poured his coffee and also poured a cup for Nathan who had accompanied him. Neither had much to say but the bond was apparent. Jay walked to the cottage for his cigarettes, found his "rocker" and took a break. After approximately fifteen minutes Jay decided to leave for Bobby's office.

He knocked on the door and Bobby invited him to enter. "Jay, I appreciate you being on time. We have a lot to discuss. We may have to break this session into two segments. We'll see how it goes and then we can decide.

First the treatment plan: Your overall progress is satisfactory regarding the specifics spelled out in your individualized treatment plan. Other staff members, who, as members of the treatment team, via the "patient record" have recorded entries regarding positive changes they have observed with you. In a way you are getting emotionally prepared to deal with the dynamics of "family week" and that is a good thing. I know you are anxious about it and the losses to your self-esteem that you have experienced, Family Week will help which starts Monday morning. Today we will formalize your discharge plan.

The plan is called a "Continuing Care Plan" because that is exactly what it is: This Continuing to Care Plan will enhance your efforts toward sustained recovery and sobriety. Treatment is but a beginning. When you exit through those double doors on the date of your discharge, the process really begins." Jay sat quietly listening intently to Bobby's words of "encouragement." That's the thought that occurred to him. Bobby was encouraging him to continue with his life and to generalize learned behaviors to society in general as he walked among those "earth people." "Jay," Bobby continued, "AA involvement will be instrumental in your continued growth and in maintaining the changes you have made. Others might say, 'Well, there's other ways to sobriety' and I have no brook with other means to achieve sobriety. I know that AA has been around since 1935 and millions of alcoholics are sober today as a direct result of their continued attendance and active participation." Jay remarked that he had talked with Tim and he had planned to attend AA post-discharge. "I'm glad to hear you say that because specifically I want you to attend 90 meetings in 90 days." "But," Jay responded, "Isn't that also feeding into my obsessive and compulsive nature: An all or none mentality!" "Not really," Bobby went on to explain. "Repetition is important immediately after a learning experience and that's what has been happening to you and for you. It is important that these newly learned skills be used immediately and the best place for that re-enforcement is through the loving, caring environment with other recovering alcoholics. Yes, 90 meetings in 90 meetings for you." "I see some of the logic in your words and since willingness is a key I will give it a try." "Fine," Bobby commented. "Continuing Care sessions are scheduled each Thursday evening from 6:00 P.M. through 7:30 P.M. They are held here and I want you to be present. After the Continuing Care session, there's an AA meeting scheduled. A temporary sponsor will be assigned and within 90 days, I will recommend that you seek a permanent sponsor. Do you know what a "sponsor's" primary responsibility is to you?" "Not really," Jay responded dryly. "Well, he is there only to offer encouragement and to help you interpret and work the 12-Steps: Period." "Oh, something like a counselor," Jay said. "Not exactly, but that's close enough for now. I have been corresponding with the City EAP who has requested that we send him a copy of Continuing Care Plan and monthly progress reports to him post-discharge." "That's fine with me, Jay answered, and I have already signed the appropriate release of information form." Bobby continued, "I am also aware of the "pro-bono" legal work you are court-ordered to complete and that will become part of your Continuing Care Plan also. I have only one more recommendation to you and that involves marital counseling. I suggest strongly that you and Kayce seek a competent therapist. If you cannot locate a suitable therapist, call me and I can make a referral for you." Bobby then sat back in his chair waiting for Jay's response.

Jay sat there looking as if a child who had been given too much homework with no time for anything else. The remark that Bobby made about marital counseling struck a nerve also. He sat thinking as Bobby poured a cup of coffee and offered a cup to Jay who gladly took it and immediately lit another cigarette. Bobby suspected that Jay needed to talk and he would provide the opportunity or maybe the "motivation." "Jay, we do need more time. I want you to consider all we have talked about and come back to my office after supper tonight and we'll finish this thing." That was fine with Jay. It was lunch time anyway. "See you about 6:00 P.M. then Jay." Jay nodded affirmatively and headed to the cafeteria with everything they had just discussed buzzing around in his mind. Jay decided that at least the ordeal would be completed by the time he went to bed tonight. Howard and Jennifer walked up and the three of them headed toward the cafeteria for lunch.

Jay was sitting in the reception area just outside Bobby's office, when Bobby walked into the room promptly at 6:00 P.M. and motioned for Jay to follow him. As they entered the office, Bobby noticed immediately how subdued Jay appeared. Jay was feeling extremely alienated. In the solitude of this alienation Jay was powerless or so he thought. Bobby chose to respond to the solitude. "Jay, the individual is endowed with two attributes that seem to ease the stressors experienced in the day-to-day affairs of living. They include 'an imagination to compensate you for what you are not and a sense of humor to console you for what you are'!" Jay nodded in agreement with an "aha" expression. Bobby continued, "The secret of successful living is not so much what happens to us but in our ability to respond appropriately to the situations that occur in our lives. Respond and that's the key word here: The ability to react and act; responsibly. Simply, you are held accountable for your actions and reactions. Perception also plays a major role in the various ways you do respond to a given situation; the way you choose to define the situation. Perception also partly defines your basic "attitudes" toward self, others, and society in general: Consider the "farmer" and the "golfer." The farmer is standing on his back porch praising the downpour of rain and the golfer is damning the downpour of rain: The same situation (rain) but entirely different responses to it. Are you with me on this?" Again Jay responded in agreement. "Are you mostly pessimistic or optimistic?" "Is the glass half-full or half-empty?" Again Jay responded with an affirmative knowing smile.

"Experience seems to teach and exhibit the fact that those individuals who are prone to addictive behaviors are by and large severely pessimistic. They take a very negative attitude toward self, others, and the world in general. Some individuals progress to develop an extremely hostile view of the world. They become distrustful, fearful and even paranoid. They are suspicious of the motives of everyone they encounter. Jay, these negative reactions combine to create chaos in your life. Your heart grows cold from within and your ability to respond appropriately disappears. Your expectations as discussed previously are cast toward the worse possible situation or outcome.

Your concerns about the upcoming family week are valid and appropriate but I strongly suggest you find a way to talk about them in the context of group. Jay, the alcoholic's intolerance for distress and the isolation and distrust that surfaces as a consequence weighs heavily for the alcoholic but it can be dramatically reduced as he gathers the courage to work honestly and openly in group. Screw your courage to the wall and go for it, Jay. They are there to listen and not to be judge and jury over a given situation. Trust the process! We have talked of trust before and let me repeat; trust me until my actions dictate otherwise. Find the way to relieve yourself of this discomfort through the group. I cannot force you to face those fears and anxieties. But I can tell you this clearly: Face the fear and the fear dies!" "I find it difficult at times to reconcile my life today, Bobby. Kayce seems so cold and distant. I want my life back and at times I do seem to "push it to the wall." Bobby did not respond waiting for the rest of it. Jay sat in silence waiting for Bobby to rescue him. That did not happen. Jay continued. "The past two and half weeks have forced me to consider my extreme behaviors especially with Kayce and Shelby." Bobby finally intervened. "Jay, your history of alcohol use and your affair with Shelby and those behaviors toward your wife cannot be corrected overnight. Perhaps family week will provide the opportunity for you and Kayce to begin the process of "mending fences." Listen, I said the "process," not resolution and not total reconciliation. Jay, slow down and consider where you are today." "I do know what you mean but it is still difficult." "Yes, it is difficult but it's worth the effort, right?" Jay again agreed. "Bobby, I know you need to get home and I really appreciate your taking this time, at this late hour, to talk with me about this."

"Continue in your quest for freedom. Trust the process and we'll talk later." Bobby got into his car and waved to Jay as he left the parking lot. Jay walked back to the cottage, stopping off for just a minute to exchange small talk with other group members.

Upon returning to his cottage, he took a quick shower and decided to call Kayce. He needed to hear her voice. As he dialed the number, his anxiety grew but he did not hang up.

Kayce answered after the fourth ring with a warm "hello." The tone of the discussion again seemed to turn cold and distant but to hear her voice cheered his sagging spirits. He didn't stay on the telephone for an extended conversation; just long enough to touch base and tell Kayce that he loved her. He gently placed the telephone receiver into its cradle and walked back out to the patio for a cigarette and a "rock" in his favorite chair.

This was meditation for him. His thoughts returned again and again to the cold and distant tone of Kayce's voice. Maybe the "Easy does it" rule does apply as Bobby stated, he thought to himself. I cannot fix this thing overnight. After finishing his cigarette, he heard several of the other group members returning from the snack bar area. They were chattering away filled with enthusiasm. For an instant Jay recognized within himself the very pessimistic attitude that always would surface (No one deserves to feel that good!). He stopped the negative process with a thought-stopping technique that Bobby had taught him. He got up from his chair and walked toward his bed. He undressed, folded his clothes neatly, and crawled into bed. He missed Kayce's touch. As he began to relax and let go, sleep took him away.

As Jay drifted further into his sleep state, the dream state began to emerge. The "Adult" goes to sleep and the "Child" emerges, alert and eager to process the day or attempt to make light of the prevailing mood prior to the "dream state." The various "children" made a decision to portray a vivid, graphic account of the unfinished business of the day. The scene would be set in the group format: The father was there, the mother was there, Kayce, Shelby, Jonathan, and Boragarde. This would do nicely. The "Adult" will walk into the room and bid each a good bye and then, tell them all good morning. A lesson will be taught to this "Adult." This simple set-up will force him to think of what he is doing to us all.

Chapter 23 – Family Week

As Kayce approached WesterBrook to begin her family week, she felt a dread welling up from the depths of her soul. She was doing just fine within the Alanon group, thanks to Mr. Melville, but she had decided that she did not belong in that collection of weird people. After her third meeting, Mr. Melville asked her to join him for a cup of coffee. After they got their cups, he approached to discuss her impending decision to quit. Kayce had looked at him in shock. "Mr. Melville, I didn't know you could read minds!" she exclaimed. He gave a full-bodied laugh and said, "Mrs. Bienville, I don't read minds a bit but I do read faces and tonight yours was shouting "escape." Then he got serious. "My dear, most of us got to this time and place in varied and different ways. How we got here doesn't really matter. It matters that you are here! You must remember that the majority of the people here have lived in the shadow of a crippling addiction for years, that is: Never being recognized, never being heard, wanting both desperately. The paradox is also being afraid of both and the truth of the matter at hand. I'll admit that the "Marla and Dottie" show sometimes is a bit much. But you must learn to weed out all of that pitch for the limelight. In spite of their theatrics, they do have some valid information for survival." Kayce interrupted, "But Mr. Melville, I am not comfortable in that group; I don't want to tell all my personal feelings to them. I am a private person and have always been so. I'm just not going to do that!" "Kayce, you don't have to. This is what I am trying to tell you. You share only what you want to share. You are a very sensitive and caring person. Share what you feel comfortable in sharing; what you feel will help someone else. The surprising thing is, simply that you will find it helping you also." Kayce looked at Mr. Melville and asked softly and earnestly: "Mr. Melville, will you be my sponsor?" "Well, Mrs. Bienville, this is highly irregular. Ordinarily, sponsors are of the same gender but in this particular case, I think it is the right thing to do. Yes, I'll be your sponsor."

Afterwards, Kayce found the Alanon meetings to be exactly what Mr. Melville said they would be. She was beginning to accept the group and feel a part of it. She was, in fact, experiencing and internalizing the first glimmer of hope for the future and her ability to accept through faith alone. Having the group available to her for support, indeed, was an added gift!

As she pulled into the WesterBrook parking lot, just the thought of Mr. Melville being there for her was fortifying and stilling her internal resolve necessary for the task ahead of her. Back to business now, she softly mumbled to herself. How is Jay going to take the news about the baby? Lord knows, I was in shock for two days!" Her thoughts immediately turned to Jon. She mentally shook herself. None of that, there will be no confessions and none to Jay or to Jon. With a sigh, she lifted her overnight bag from the car. Someone would have to help her with the rest. As she approached the door, a young man was leaving and held it open for her. In the lobby, she introduced herself and was asked to be seated. In a short while a perky young lady named Connie appeared and introduced herself as a "Patient Service Representative" and asked Kayce to follow her. Connie led her to a nicely furnished room that held two twin beds. Kayce looked questioningly at Connie. Connie smiled and confirmed that she would, indeed, have a roommate. Connie told her that shortly someone would come assist her with the remaining baggage.

Kayce selected her bed, the one next to the window, and sat down on it. She was deep in her own thoughts and was not immediately aware that Connie had brought another woman into the room. "Kayce, Kayce!" Connie was calling her name. "Yes, Connie." "Kayce, this is Bonnie. You and Bonnie will be rooming with each other this week." Kayce stood up to meet the vivacious blonde standing in front of her.

Bonnie was petite, fair, blue eyed and silvery blonde. It was apparent that her lovely hair did not come from a bottle. She was slender for such a short person and had a very engaging smile. "Hi, I'm Kayce." Bonnie seemed to relax and said, "Geeze, I'm glad you're young. I was afraid they would room me with a really old woman. So, Kayce, what do'ya think we're in for, I mean, what do'ya think they are gonna do to us? I'm here because of Howard, that's my old man. I love'em, so I'm here." Kayce pondered Bonnie's question and silently added one of her own, exactly why am I here? She couldn't answer her own question but said to Bonnie, "I have no idea, Bonnie. I suppose we will have to wait and see."

At that point, Connie stuck her head in the door and told them they had ten minutes before orientation and that two aides were in the lobby to assist them, if they needed to get additional baggage out of their cars. Kayce and Bonnie took the offer of help and had just enough time to get their remaining baggage in the room and then get to the group room in time for the beginning of the orientation session. As they sat down Bonnie said to Kayce with a wry smile, "Looks like we're about to have our week planned out for us." Kayce smiled back and nodded.

At that moment, a neatly dressed lady who looked like someone's grandmother introduced herself: "Hello everyone, I'm Margaret Doddy, Director of Family Services here at WesterBrook. I'm usually called Dr. Doddy (that's PhD, not MD) but there are some here who call me Doddering Doddy!" She laughed and said, "I prefer you call me

Margaret. I want to welcome each of you to WesterBrook and assure you we are here to help you. Call extension 3378 and my secretary will arrange an appointment for you. Now let me introduce you to your family group leader." "Ladies and gentlemen, this is Kevin Kerdson. Kevin has a Masters Degree in Social Work and a Masters in Family Counseling." "Thank you, Dr. Doddy".

As he turned his attention to the group, he said, "Hello, everyone. I'm Kevin and I am looking forward to sharing this next week with you. We have some hard work ahead of us but we will see it through. Look to your front, now to your back, right side, and left side. Notice, you are surrounded with people who share common ground with you. You do not know these people yet but you will in ways that will bolster your spirits indeed. You will also recognize clearly that you are not alone in this therapy room or the world at large. This isn't a "me" thing, it is a "we" thing! And we can do it! Now if you will look at the paper you picked up out of your chair before you sat down, you will see that it is an agenda for this week."

Kayce looked over at Bonnie who was feverishly trying to "iron out" the paper she had folded into a fan. Kayce's spirits lifted slightly. Silently, she laughed. Bonnie was like an irrepressible child. She was a blessing to Kayce and Kayce realized that lighthearted Bonnie had been specifically assigned to her by her guardian angel. She turned her attention to Kevin who was beginning to outline the week ahead. After Kevin finished the agenda for the week, Kayce and Bonnie went back to their room.

Bonnie was sitting on the bed with a perplexed look on her face. "Ya know Kayce, I don't know about this education stuff. I never was too good in school. Just barely got by, if you know what I mean. Do they mean we gotta study and take tests and all that stuff?" "Well, Bonnie, Kayce began, I don't think it will be exactly like school. I think they just want us to know about the disease of addiction, you know, just the facts about it: Facts without any emotional attachments so we can see it clearly. Also Kevin said this week was to help us get beyond feeling responsible for our loved ones' addictions and to be able to get a grip on our lives." Bonnie gave a sigh of relief. "Well, girlfriend, I surely could use some help there!"

It was dinner time so Kayce and Bonnie went to the cafeteria. Kayce was surprised to see Jay crossing the cafeteria with his tray in hand. She studied him as he came toward her. He looked better than he had looked in years. The tense look about him was gone and his eyes shown clear. Momentarily, she was eleven again and thought of his brown eyes shining with golden flecks.

As he sat down, Bonnie and Howard moved to another table for a little privacy not only for Jay and Kayce but also for themselves too. Tentatively, Kayce said: "I didn't know we were going to eat dinner together tonight." For an instant there was a disappointed look on Jay's face but immediately it was gone. "Well, we all usually eat together, I mean family and patients but if you would rather be alone, I can move to another table. I know how the first night here can be and understand if you want solitude." Kayce looked deep into Jay's eyes and said "No, I want you to stay. I just didn't know that it was allowed." Jay smiled in relief. "As a matter of fact, I am glad we are alone because I have something to tell you and I think, no, I know, a husband and wife should share this kind of news with only each other first." Jay looked very puzzled and interested but it was obvious that he did not pick up on the clues Kayce had given him. He waited with an expectant look on his face.

Softly Kayce said: "Jay, we are going to have a baby: I am two months pregnant." A baby was just mentioned leaving

Jay to doubt his senses: A baby? He was elated despite the timing! And despite this wonderful news, his thoughts went immediately to the things he had been told in the early weeks of his treatment and one of them was no major changes in your life in the first two years of sobriety: Talking about a major change! He realized that there had been a few minutes silence and looked up to see Kayce's green eyes searching his face. She smiled at him. "It's okay Jay, not to be real thrilled right now. I understand. I was somewhat overwhelmed myself. I just wanted to share this with you and only you first." Jay continued in the joyfulness that he was experiencing and responded to his wife. "Kayce, you have given me a renewed sense of well-being, of being sober, of being your husband, of being a father to our child, and of being your best friend. We now have a new life to consider and I am pleased with this news even though I might be hallucinating! Jay was amused at his remark yet he clearly communicated to Kayce that they would be good parents!" Both had lost their appetites but Kayce made herself eat. Nutrition was important to her now. As dinner ended, they walked over to the area where trays were emptied and Jay placed theirs on the conveyor to the kitchen. He walked her to the lobby, leaned over and kissed her on the cheek. "See you tomorrow Kayce." As she managed a smile, Kayce walked back to her room.

She lay down on her bed and began to cry. This man is a stranger to me now, she thought. How am I ever going to rebuild a life with him? Doesn't he know how much I am hurting? She did not hear Bonnie when she came into the room. She felt a hand on her shoulder and heard Bonnie say softly: "You okay, honey"? Kayce nodded and Bonnie had the good sense to leave her alone and go over to her bed and read a magazine.

Family week progressed and each day Kayce learned more and more about the disease of addiction and how she became a "co-dependent person." Mornings were spent in group with Kevin and other family members. They had lectures on alcoholism and drug addiction. They had group discussions which got quite lively but after one particularly upsetting confrontation for Kayce, she called her doctor who immediately contacted the treatment team and explained that Kayce was in her first trimester of pregnancy and that it was imperative that she not become unduly upset. After Kevin gently admonished her for not sharing her good news with the group, he and the group members were gentler with her and her family week moved along. Afternoons were spent in conference with Jay and his counselor.

One afternoon Kayce was encouraged to confront Jay with her feelings about his alcoholic behavior. Kayce shared her fear of the physical abuse and her anger at the affair with Shelby. She shared her disappointment that Jay had a daughter whom he did not acknowledge to her. Another afternoon Jay was encouraged to confront Kayce with his feelings about her enabling, about how her silence at times made him feel shut out of her life just as he had felt shut out of his parents' lives.

During the week Kayce had learned that the excuses, lies, and other things she did to cover up Jay's alcoholism contributed to the worsening of it. At the end of Family Week, Kayce left WesterBrook feeling much better about herself and Jay. She still wasn't sure where their relationship was headed but at least it seemed to have turned the corner and was headed in a new direction. Driving away from WesterBrook, she recalled an Alanon saying "one day at a time" and that was how she was going to do it. Her thoughts turned to Bonnie. Bonnie was the most unlikely candidate for a friend but a firm and fast friendship had developed. The farewell to all of the family group members was emotional. The goodbye to Bonnie was really tough. Each had left with the other's address and phone number. Kayce was determined to keep in touch with Bonnie. For the first time in years Kayce knew everything was going to be okay. Whatever the outcome of things, she had the beginnings of a serenity that would see her through it.

Chapter 24 – Onward to Live in Freedom

This was the day Jay had been looking forward to for almost four weeks but now that it was here, he felt a sadness surrounding the event. It reminded him of what Bobby said about one door closing and another door opening for him. He had developed an emotional, living closeness with this group and he had grown as a consequence of that closeness. He felt attached to a living and breathing process. He was experiencing the separation anxiety of the child just as Bobby had counseled in one of his earlier sessions.

He had been part of this ceremony before as others prepared to leave the group but it certainly felt different being the one leaving. He fully recognized that accepting that gate-symbol from Bobby and his fellow group members had a dual purpose: To a commitment to his personal journey of recovery in taking those steps as he navigated through the rough waters that would hinder him occasionally, and, to the group members, as a group, would remain his bulwark of recovery through unity of purpose and unity of living. His group and the consciousness of that group would forever remain in his memory. And half of the battle would be charted and the rest would be his alone to navigate.

As everyone took their seats, Bobby opened the group as on countless other days and it seemed good just to hear the voice that he now "trusted" completely and without reservations. Bobby was indeed a special man. His caring, his compassionate nature, his non-judgmental attitude, and his consistency in all matters, came across clearly in every contact. The beginning ceremony was called a "discharge evaluation" and it involved every member of the group as they shared with Jay passing the gate-symbol from one set of hands to the next. The last to pass the gate-symbol to Jay was

Bobby. Bobby took the shiny gate-symbol and invited Jay to the center of the group. "You have made substantial progress during the short time you've been here at WesterBrook. Just as you found the practice of law in the real world far different from that taught within the ivy covered halls of the curriculum of jurisprudence, so you will find your efforts to maintain sobriety in the world outside these doors. You have been given the steps to your sobriety and now put them on the gate-symbol presented to you today by your group and use them daily. Jay, just as I promised in the beginning, I have walked along beside you encouraging you at times but never dragging you, kicking and screaming. Remember those difficult first days and your endless episodes of extreme anxiety. Don't forget the gains you've made. Don't forget us. I will always remember how hard you have worked. I now want to extend to you the invitation to experience the joy and freedom that recovery and sobriety can provide." Bobby then hugged Jay heartily and both returned to their respective seats.

Bobby's eyes reddened and so did Jay's. "Now, Jay, you may have the floor to share your thoughts with your group," Bobby added caringly. Jay's voice began to gently break as he told his fellow group members of his deep appreciation for their personal caring and concern including their abiding supportive attitude. This had been an experience that he would never forget. He related to the idea of Confucius, which helped him to further praise his fellow group members: "I hear and I forget," "I see and I remember," "I do and I understand".

The group sat as if hypnotized by Jay's remarks. Bobby and Janice remained silent allowing Jay to have his say. Jay continued.

He wanted those who would remain after he left the group to share in his growth experience. He told of a recognition that life "is" at times unfair and unjust and that ultimately, speaking in the existential sense, that there is no escape from some of life's pains and sufferings. Even though it is a "we proposition," it is important to recognize that no matter how close he would get to others, he must still face life alone. It was at this point that Jay recalled a statement made by one of his philosophy professors: Two things you do very much alone; one is being born and the other is dying. What you do with the time between these events is pretty much your choice. He would make the right choice for himself and his recovery. The support of others in the process of recovery is extremely important in the quality of sobriety that he would enjoy.

He had been given many "gifts" during his treatment experience and one that had been given him was the courage to face those very basic issues of life and death thus learning to live his life more honestly and being less caught up in life's trivialities. His treatment experience had brought a clarity of what was truly important and worthy of his time and energy today. Much of what was obsessed-upon in the past would be dropped in favor of developing meaningful relationships with significant others in his life resulting in the fulfillment of certain promises made to him. He had further gained the understanding that he must take ultimate responsibility for the way he lives his life no matter how much guidance and support he would receive from others. He recognized further that "an easy does it" attitude must prevail in his recovery efforts and he wanted to convey that subtle message to his group.

Jay was internalizing a finely tuned awareness of the world and of himself. The world no longer revolved around him. He was gaining a better understanding of life's dilemmas, both good and not so good, and within that process he would be better able to cope more appropriately rather than returning to a chemical. He had also begun to realize another aspect of himself: That he was addicted to fooling himself. His addictive behavior would always be a part of him but through the experience of treatment, his loving and caring group members, and his counselor, he would be able to channel his addictive energies into more appropriate actions and reactions. A thought crossed his mind that in the very beginning he had ideas of running from all of this. Of just dumping his treatment, his career, his marriage and throwing it all away but today he was a new man. He would always be grateful for the gifts that he had been given. Perhaps one day he could repay the debt he could never repay and perhaps he could, because he was no longer a lost child and there was more to life after all.

"I want to express my deep abiding faith in the process which has provided me a new set of living skills that I shall never forget," Jay said to the group.

Bobby thanked Jay for his timely remarks and other members in the group were beaming with authentic self-pride. "This thing works as always," Bobby thought. And he recalled his early days of group when he felt compelled to take an active, directive stance through confronting all defenses exhibited by members of the group. But Bobby knew that the highly dedicated and experienced counselor knew when to tighten the reins and when to release them. He further knew that with every goodbye from one of his patients he had learned ever so slowly to feel the subtle difference between chaining a soul and holding a hand. Life indeed is a circle of hope as members are admitted and members are discharged back to the world.

Another group session concluded as the group members joined hands and recited the Serenity Prayer: "God, Grant me the Serenity to accept the things I cannot change, the courage to change the things I can, and the Wisdom to know the difference." Afterward, hugs were exchanged and the hallway then filled with a mass of bodies again headed toward the cafeteria.

Jay completed the day's events and looked forward to retiring to his last night of rest at WesterBrook. After this day's events and his discharge from WesterBrook being scheduled for 9:00 AM, Jay's thoughts turned inward as he reflected upon and considered the transformations he had experienced in the past four weeks of his life. His resentment toward his father had faded into a warm, forgiving feeling because he had followed the suggestion of Bobby regarding prayers being extended for his father. He knew a conversation with his father would bring the relationship he had sought for so many years. His anger that had been used to cover-up his "deep-seated hurts" had been exposed to the light of reason.

He found himself experiencing feelings he thought had long been forgotten. Emotionally, yes, he was alive but now how to control the torrent of feelings that begged for expression. Sitting in his rocker on the cottage patio with everyone else in bed, his tears flowed as he considered his life. Thoughts of the Kayce he knew long ago continued to sweep over him. Shelby. Marianne. Jay knew self-pity and rightly so. This was not self-pity but a re-awakening as the Steps had promised him. And Jay knew that tonight. He heard the sounds of the night around him, felt the wind lightly blowing across the patio and considered the vast universe and all its inter-connectedness. Never before had he considered such trivial matters, but for now these things did matter and more importantly, they mattered to him. He felt wondrously alive! He would put his thoughts on paper for Bobby and mail his thanks to him. Never in his wildest dreams did he ever think he could feel the way he did tonight. Thankfulness and a sense of profound gratitude pervaded his every thought now but how to extend these wonderful feelings to those who had facilitated this new awareness? He would try to find a way to do that, and more, with his recovery one day at a time. He was getting deliciously tired and sleepy and headed for his bed. Tomorrow would be a big day for him and hopefully for Kayce as well. As he lay there, his dream was revealed and sleep enveloped him as his tears dried on his cheeks.

EPILOGUE

Kayce sat on the terrace steps and watched Jay play with Marianne and Jaque. Marianne was five and Jaque was almost three. Marianne was tall and dark, like her Father. Jaque, in contrast, looked like a golden haired cherub. He was a joy to Kayce. It hardly seemed over two years had passed since Jay was discharged from WesterBrook. Although their treatment team had suggested no major changes in their lives for a couple of years, Kayce's pregnancy was a happy occasion. She found out about the baby while Jay was in treatment. Not much could be done about it, and Kayce didn't want to do anything about it. A peal of laughter drew her attention to the three romping in the grass. Marianne was tickling Jaque. Kayce couldn't say she had completely forgiven Shelby but all the bitterness was gone. And she was truly thankful for Marianne's relationship with Jay. The child was an innocent party and Kayce held no malice for her.

Her thoughts turned to Jay. A gentle wave of affection flooded over her. Jay was growing in his sobriety. Kayce thought about the two years continuing care commitment she and Jay agreed to upon his discharge from WesterBrook. At first, every Thursday night was a hassle but after a while, she and Jay began to look forward to the sessions. The only one they missed was the Thursday night Jacque was born. However, the next week, they were there. As a matter of fact, even though the two year commitment period had passed, they still managed to attend a Thursday night session at least once a month. This was a part of their life now and they were not about to give it up! Immediately, she felt pity for him. Poor Jay, he would never know what his addiction had cost him. The passionate love she once felt for him was only a distant memory. It had died and had been replaced with a love that had the qualities of a long, fast friendship. This would be enough for Kayce and she knew this marriage would last. Her thoughts turned to Jon. In his last letter, he actually sounded happy. Kayce feverously hoped the relationship with the Alaskan girl would turn into the kind of love Jon deserved. Kayce looked toward Jaque and smiled softly. For once she was very grateful for her fairness of hair and complexion. There was no need to explain Jacque's fair hair and ruddy complexion.

Jay had begged the children for a rest and was leaning against the stately magnolia tree. Marianne and Jacque were still playing. Their childish laughter was music to his ears. He glanced over at Kayce. Once again he thought to himself what an extraordinary woman she was. There were tense moments early in his sobriety. The bridge building had taken a long time. The family encounter at WesterBrook had been less than successful because of Kayce's pregnancy. The first session had been extremely upsetting for her. When she returned, it was with the news of the expected baby and doctor's orders that it would not be in her or the baby's best interest to repeat such an ordeal. After the initial shock, Kayce was so enthralled with the impending motherhood that she simply withdrew if she felt that anything was threatening her well being. However, Mr. Melville, a fellow Alanon member, came to Kayce's rescue. Gently, but firmly, he guided Kayce through the turbulent waters of living with a newly recovering person. He also helped Kayce to understand her actions and motives better, and the part she had played in Jay's addiction. Mr. Melville remains a vital part of our life. He and Miss Lucy are a third set of grandparents for Jacque and Marianne.

Jay looked over at Marianne. The way Kayce had accepted her was amazing. Of course, Kayce did not have a vindictive bone in her lovely body. When Kayce had gotten home from the hospital after her collapse during the court, Jay was afraid he was going to lose her. It was four weeks before Kayce approached him concerning Shelby. She sat across from him in the den looking like a pale golden angel. Jay started to speak and Kayce had simply silenced him with an upraised hand. "Jay I don't want to hear any excuses for your affair with Shelby. There is nothing you can say that will justify that sordid affair. There is no room for negotiation or concession on my part. Here is what must be if you and I are to remain married. You will end the relationship at once. The only contact you will have with Shelby will be concerning Marianne and that contact will be in this home with me present or at our attorney's with him present. The decisions you and Shelby make concerning your daughter will be yours alone. I will not interfere but you will not be alone with Shelby. Secondly, you will have Walton draw up the necessary papers to give Marianne the Bienville name and she will be allowed to take her place in this family. You will see legally, you have joint custody of the child. She needs to be exposed to life outside of the characters she has come in contact with at Buddes. These two conditions must be met before we can consider mending our relationship. I'm not sure it can be mended but I know for a fact these two things must happen. There is no discussion to be had at this time, Jay. Think about it and let me know!"

Later, Jay called Walton and Shelby and made arrangements. Kayce and Shelby would meet with the attorney the next day. He was surprised at how readily Shelby agreed to everything. Jay was told that Shelby had a married a computer programmer and they were expecting a child any day. She no longer worked at Buddes and she seemed extremely happy. He hoped she was.

His life seemed to have come full circle. He realized he, too, was happy and content. Only rarely now did his Kayce seem in some distant memory he could not visit. His quest was to help her reach the time when she forgot whatever it was that separated her from him in those brief seconds.

As Jay stood up and stepped into the sunlight, he saw Kayce walking toward him, at long last, he knew! Every day in his continuing recovery held the promise of another. At last Jay was freed from his inordinate fears, the terrible pangs of guilt, and of the deep remorse that at one time haunted him so. He was finally free! As he reflected upon the past six months, those tears that once frightened him and left him out of control were now a welcomed guest within his soul. Yes, he knew and he would remember!

Post-Script

Addiction to alcohol and other mood/mind altering drugs is characterized by depths of loneliness, emotional and physical isolation, and a constant internalized feeling of being "less than"; being "apart from" rather than "a part of". Recovery is moving beyond the pain of addiction and sustaining the new perspective gained through the treatment process guided by the recognition and acceptance that internal change and flexibility in the "life process" brings a new focused direction to life. Recovery is the ultimate goal of the process of treatment being reflective of a change brought about by a refocus of energies involving the physical, emotional, mental, and spiritual aspects of the individual. Webster's dictionary defines the word "recover" as "to begin anew". In treatment for addictions, recovery is to "begin anew". It is the ongoing process of "recovering"; i.e., regaining and rebuilding that wholeness of being. Recovery is also the lifetime rediscovery of ourselves as well as new explorations of parts of us we never knew existed. It is the ever-widening comfort zone, which brings interpersonal and intrapersonal harmony. But more importantly, recovery is "Sobriety". This "sobriety" encompasses clarity of thought with a self-confidence that needs no inflated ego to function soberly.

Sobriety exists and attaining it and maintaining it has a price also. You must work and strive as hard as you did to maintain your active addiction! I honor all who attempt this journey to a new life in sobriety because you have now begun the process of destroying denial that perpetuated the addiction in your life!

Treatment works for those who work for it.

LIST OF SIGNIFICANT OTHERS

Delta Dubois – Southern Heritage Reporter

Jeninne Bienville – Jay's Mother

Charles Phillip Bienville – Jay's Father

Louisa Mathers – Personal secretary to Jeninne Bienville

Greta Baxley – Serving Maid to Jeninne Bienville

Ms Nesbitt – "Nanny"

Jay Bienville – Alcoholic Attorney – the patient

Kayce Bienville – Wife of Jay

Macklin Devere – Psychiatrist

Shelby Longmire – The other woman

Jonathan Moreau – Friend of Jay's

Tommy Venerable – Private Investigator

Jericho Townsend – Sheriff of Trace Parish

Judge Lashley Holloway – Presiding Judge

Walton Pierce – Jay's Attorney

Jean Johnson – Monique's Attorney

Thomas Writon – Assessment Diagnostician

Sherry – Staff Aide

Bobby Gandaff- Primary Counselor

Janice Bibiak – Group Co-Facilitator

Jeremy Daniels – Program Director

Ron Price – Medical Director

Tim Wilson – AA presenter

Karl Goshin – Chaplain

Marianne – Jay and Shelby's daughter

Beatrice (Bea) – Kayce's Housekeeper

Kevin Kerdson – Family Therapist

Margaret Doddy – Family Services Supervisor

The Group: Shane, Jennifer, Rene, Howard, Gayland, David, Jackson, and Janet

ABOUT THE AUTHOR

The Author has been involved with mental health and addiction treatment since 1984. He has been retired since 2007. He earned his Undergraduate Degree from the University of Tennessee (Business Administration), his Masters Degree from Troy University (Counseling and Human Development), and his PhD from Century University (Educational Psychology). He has been married to Elizabeth since 1981. She has been in his heart since he was 12-years old!